LETTERS
TO A
DYING
FRIEND

LETTERS
TO A
DYING
FRIEND

Helping Those You Love
Make a Conscious Transition

ANTON GROSZ, PH.D.

A publication supported by
THE KERN FOUNDATION

Quest Books
Theosophical Publishing House

Wheaton, Illinois ♦ Chennai (Madras), India

First Quest Edition 1989
Revised Edition 1997

The Theosophical Publishing House
P.O. Box 270
Wheaton, IL 60189-0270

A publication of the Theosophical Publishing House,
a department of the Theosophical Society in America

Library of Congress Cataloging-in-Publication Data

Grosz, Anton.
    Letters to a dying friend; helping those you love make a
conscious transition / Anton Grosz -- Rev. ed.
        p.   cm. -- (Quest Books)
    "A publication supported by the Kern Foundation."
    Includes bibliographical references.
    ISBN 0-8356-0765-8
    1. Future life.   2. Death--Religious aspects.   3. Karma-
glin-pa, 14th cent.   Bar do thos grol.   4. Death--Religious
aspects--Buddhism.   5 Intermediate state--Buddhism.
    I. Kern Foundation.   II. Title
    BL535.G76   1997
    291.2'3--dc21
                                                            97-22259
                                                            CIP

Interior art by Alice Topf.

6 5 4 3 2 1 ° 97 98 99 00 01 02

Printed in the United States of America

Contents

Foreword by
H. H. The Dalai Lama

Death is a process which will come to all of us. What we cannot be sure of is when it will strike, or what will follow. Many people find the mystery and uncertainty associated with death frightening, and they pretend it does not exist or at least will not befall them. However, a realistic acceptance of death is healthy, because it stimulates a greater appreciation of the value of our lives.

If we could prove that at death we simply stop, like a candle burning out, then we might simply seek to enjoy ourselves while we can. However, mankind has long suspected some sort of life after death. Indeed, a beginningless succession of lives is a fundamental teaching of Buddhism, while in the Tantric tradition adept meditators have explored the process of death and even transformed it into a means for gaining enlightenment. Of the many Tibetan works describing the process, the *Bardo Thödol* or *Liberation Through Hearing in the Intermediate State* has become well known in translation as *The Tibetan Book of the Dead*. Recently, its description of what happens at death has received some verification from the corresponding accounts of people who have died and been resuscitated. So, death is a reality which we cannot prevent, and there is existence after it. What can we do? For most of us ordinary people who lead busy lives, what is more important is to develop a generous kind heart towards others. If we can do that and live accordingly, we will be able to die peacefully and without regret. A few who have the opportunity and the necessary circumstances, such as a qualified teacher, may engage in the practice of yoga and achieve higher spiritual accomplishments.

Anton Grosz's *Letters to a Dying Friend* is addressed to us all; its underlying message is that we are all going to die, and with that in mind we should now put our lives to the best use we can.

Preface

Four years ago my friend Peter died. One moment he was jogging with his German shepherd, Max, through the sculptured gardens of the Olana estate in upstate New York; the next moment he was dead—and the world had lost a beautiful soul.

At the funeral the main point, made over and over as if to give comfort both to those hearing and saying it, was that death had been so mercifully sudden that there could not have been any suffering. In one sense, this was true. Peter had been in the best of health up until the instant he keeled over in mid-stride. He ate well and in moderation, exercised regularly, watched his cholesterol, and, as the administrator of Columbia Memorial Hospital and a colonel in the Air Force Reserve, had his annual physical examinations. His death could not have caused him anything more than a microsecond of physical pain, if that.

And there had been no mental suffering, either. Peter loved life and he lived it to the hilt, right up to the very end. He had not had to listen to stern-faced doctors tell him of incurable disease, nor had he been forced to limit his activities, or live his final days under the shadow of imminent death. Yes, Peter had been lucky. For though he may have died young, he died well. He died easily. And yet something bothered me.

For a number of years I had run into a stone wall in trying to share with Peter my interest in life beyond the body, in "what happens next" after we die. It's not that the opportunity wasn't there. As members of "The Brotherhood," a barbershop quartet that performed throughout the United States and Canada, we virtually lived with each other two weekends a month for five years, not to mention the time spent at weekly rehearsals. Along with the other two quartet members, we often found ourselves stuck together on long car rides or sitting in airports waiting to make connecting flights. When our voices had grown tired from singing, or we had temporarily run out of ideas for new show routines, we would discuss our business careers, our families, our interests, and our thoughts.

Every now and then the subject would get around to my personal out-of-body experiences and the research I was undertaking relating modern death return experiences with the scenario presented by the ancient and mysterious Tibetan *Bardo Thödol*. Sometimes Peter wouldn't even listen. "When you can prove it to me in black and white," he would say, "when you can bring something back with you that I can see or touch, then I'll believe you. Meanwhile, there are enough things that science can prove to keep me busy."

His refusal to open himself to even the possibility of an inner world, invisible to the senses and existing independently of the body, only spurred my desire to further communicate things I not only accepted, but which had literally changed my life. And it wasn't ego, a desire to override his will, or to prove my point that provided my main motivation. Rather, it was the fact that Peter was my friend, my dear friend, and I truly believed that what I had to say would benefit him sometime in the distant future.

I decided to take a more tactical approach and stopped discussing the topic with the group, while at the same time I worked to arrange my material into a coherent logical format. I would marshal my information and present it all at once in a manner which Peter could not help but accept as real, even if he should choose not to use these findings in his personal life.

In August 1984 the first draft was finished. I would give him a copy the next time we got together. But life is truly stranger than fiction, and my well-laid plan never came to pass. The day after the draft was completed, I received the phone call telling me of Peter's sudden and unexpected death. He died thirty years before he should have, and as a result, my efforts were one day too late.

I've meditated a lot since then, on life and death and who we truly are and what our roles are on this planet and beyond. It is now clear to me that my role, at least at this point in my life, is to share all the information I have been privileged to receive concerning consciousness, the soul, and life beyond death—the very information I wanted so much to share with my friend Peter.

It is all written down on the following pages in the form of short letters addressed simply "Dear friend." They could just as easily have been addressed "Dear Peter," for I often do see him in my mind's eye as I sit at the computer letting the words flow through me. But it would not be real. Peter can no longer be reached through the printed word.

However, you can. You are alive and can yet benefit from new knowledge concerning life beyond death, the soul, and ultimate reality. My research, my studies, my life work are all for you, my friend, for it is your presence that now gives them meaning. Accept my words as they are given, with love. For I honestly believe everything I tell you to be true, and I honestly believe that you will benefit from the telling.

I share with you all I have, and wish you peace and light and love, from this day forth, even for evermore.

Dear Caregiver to the Dying,

It is fascinating. Normally, about 20 percent of the people in my workshops can recall personal out-of-body or death return experiences. This is somewhat above the national average of 10 to 15 percent. But in classes for those who work with the dying, home care nurses, hospice volunteers, and the like, the number is well over 50 percent. I don't think this is just coincidence.

Could it be that one's own personal experience beyond the veil is a driving reason for choosing to work with the dying? Could it be that when one knows for certain that life beyond death is a reality, one also knows how important it is to give love and aid at the time of death when it is so greatly needed?

These days the subject of life after death is shedding its taboo-like aura and becoming part of our mass culture, being discussed without hushed tones and raised eyebrows. Oh, there have always been tales of ghosts and spirits that haunted cemeteries, and yes, Scrooge encountered Marley's ghost and the spirits of Christmas past, present, and future. But that was considered fiction, not a reflection on nonphysical reality.

Recently, Hollywood, which not only mirrors the attitudes of mass culture but greatly influences it, has produced a number of movies dealing with life after death and reincarnation. Not counting *Topper* done back in 1937, this recent interest was rekindled in 1979 with *Heaven Can Wait*, produced interestingly enough by Warren Beatty, Shirley MacLaine's brother. (Who says spirituality doesn't run in families?) And though such movies as *Ghost, Always, Made In Heaven, Chances Are,* and *Defending Your Life* may not agree on the details of the afterlife realm, nevertheless they all depict life after death, not as something strange and spooky, but as something very real and natural that we will all have to face someday in one form or another, regardless of our beliefs.

We are also seeing Death Return Experiences on prime-time television. In one case the star of a detective series was shot and died. While doctors worked on his body in the hospital, he traveled to various nonphysical places, met his parents who had died years before, and was given a choice of whether to return to earth. Of course he chose to return, just before the hour was up.

This scenario may not be profound, but there it was on prime-time television, reaching the very core of American society with the message that there is something to life after death after all. Clearly we are becoming more open to the reality of life beyond the body at the very time that modern science and ancient teachings are pointing in a similar direction. This development is very exciting, for there is no question that a society that believes in life beyond death is a very different society from one that does not.

One consequence of this belief is a rethinking of the right to die. Should people be forced to live if they wish to escape the pain of a terminal illness? Should machines keep the bodies of patients in a vegetative state alive after there is agreement that there is no consciousness inside? Such issues will be resolved differently in societies which accept life beyond the body and those that do not.

The time is also ripe for those who are aware of the truth to share that truth with others, though this doesn't require getting up on a soapbox to preach. It just means sharing experiences when the opportunity arises or being the first to say "reincarnation" or "out-of-body." A person who does so may find someone else, possibly a patient, who has been waiting to share his or her own experience but has been afraid. Every time I do a radio talk show someone always calls in to tell of an experience from years ago that had never been revealed for fear of ridicule. Often, the person just needed to hear someone say it first in order to "come out of the closet," as it were.

We are just beginning to understand and use non-physical methods such as therapeutic touch in the care and treatment of patients. We may not know why or how these methods work, but as Einstein said, that's the difference between theory and practice. When you know what's supposed to happen but it doesn't work, that's theory. When something works but you don't know why, that's practice.

In your work with the dying, you can check with your patients about the nature of their dreams. Are there dreams of bridges or crossings or doors or gates? One hospice worker was told by her patient, "I keep having this dream where I'm trying to jump to the other side." The next day he died. The dream was a clear indication that he was ready to let go. Also see if there are any dreams about lights. Ask if they are bright lights or dim lights, and what color they are. The significance of these lights is discussed in this book.

Remember that the subject of life after death touches on religion, and offense can be taken when ideas are presented in a sectarian manner. However, this need not occur, for the reality is that life after death exists for all regardless of the path they have taken in life. The teachings shared in this book can be incorporated into all belief systems. No one is saying, "You must believe what I say, or else!" You and your patients are free to take or not to take these ideas as you choose.

Finally, from a personal point of view, it is a pleasure to share this material. You caregivers are in the forefront of the new awareness; you are creating the climate and atmosphere of love and caring which is the hallmark of coming generations, and I honor you for your work. I regret only the disproportion of males to females involved in care for the dying. Someday I hope there will be more men who have the feeling and empathy so abundant in women, which enables them to share and give of themselves at this most important time of life.

Peace and Love,
Anton Grosz
August 28, 1991

Dear friend,
    A lot has happened since *Letters* was first published in 1989. Spurred on by an unchecked AIDS epidemic, a violent society where senseless killing is nightly news, and a medical system based more on profit than concern for the patient, death as a subject for discussion has finally come out of the closet.
    And it has been more that just talk. Organizations have sprung up around the country to assist the dying make the great transition. Laws opposing physician assisted death for terminally ill patients have, in some cases, been declared unconstitutional, and a renegade doctor has captured national headlines by treating the dying as human beings whose wishes should be honored.
    Even insurance companies, far from the most compassionate segment of our society, have devised plans

that allow the terminally ill to tap into life insurance policies so as to use stored up resources to provide needed care during their final days. Underlying all of this is the growing acceptance that death is a part of life, something we must all face one day, and that it is simply not intelligent to make its discussion a societal taboo.

In the larger scheme of things, I think it is not mere coincidence that this newfound recognition of death as an integral part of life has also paralleled the diaspora of the Tibetan people throughout the world. For over a thousand years, while we in the West have studied the physical body and the world outside, Tibetan scholars, living isolated lives at the top of the world, have studied the metaphysical body and the world within. Their national tragedy in being exiled from their country has had the benefit of bringing their profound knowledge of life beyond the death of the body to the attention of the rest of us. It is about time.

Meanwhile the practice of medicine has added to the growing knowledge of life after death by its ability to resuscitate patients after longer and longer periods of clinically defined death. The reports of those having such experiences, chronicled in numerous case studies, have verified milestones the Tibetans describe as existing along the way.

And a surprising and allied movement supporting the reality of life after death has also come from unexpected scientific quarters. The latest findings of quantum physics seem to show that consciousness and not matter is actually the ultimate ground of being. This would imply that awareness can exist without being encased in a physical body, quite the reverse from the old materialist view that stated that once the body dies consciousness ceases as well.

The importance of this issue lies not in scientific or

philosophical posturing, nor in finger pointing as to whose view is right and whose is wrong. Rather, it is in the practical and undeniable fact that each of us alive today is one day going to die. And if we suspect that there is a continuity of awareness existing beyond the demise of the body, we would be fools to live our embodied lives as if this were not the case.

Clearly, we are at one of those critical points in history where the paradigm is shifting and new understandings of reality are becoming the norm. And just as we look back to the days when people thought the Sun circled a flat Earth, so may humans in the not so distant future look back on our views of life and death and wonder how we could have been so primitive.

Peace and Love,
Anton Grosz, Ph.D.
San Francisco, June 1996

Acknowledgments

This work is dedicated to the memory of Peter Donatelli and all the beautiful souls in the universe. May it bring peace and comfort to all who read it and may its words be remembered when they are most needed.

Special thanks to my wife Phyllis, my children Gerald and Danielle, my sister Julie, and my friend Ron Rozman for their support in this project. And of course, highest homage to the Tibetan people for keeping this information alive for these thousands of years. May the publication of this, our joint effort, be for the benefit of all sentient beings.

Om Shanti Shanti Shanti

Introduction

If books are any indication of our national psyche, we have come some distance since Ernest Becker's memorable work, *The Denial of Death*. One need only mention the pioneering efforts of Elisabeth Kübler Ross, the host of books on the near-death experience, and the worldwide network of Dr. Gerald Jampolsky's Centers for Attitudinal Healing (the attitude needing healing being our attitude toward death).

Letters to a Dying Friend is a valuable contribution, and in a class by itself. It is an elucidation of a most obscure work, little known in the west—the *Tibetan Book of the Dead*. Through a series of beautiful simple letters, Anton Grosz makes this strange and ancient text readily accessible to any reader. There is real learning for us here.

How dreadfully unprepared we humans seem to be for the series of circumstances that befalls us. We are dropped into the world at birth—helpless and unsuspecting; we are plunged into adolescence seriously unprepared to cope with the vast new forces at work within and around us; and we enter into adult life—the workplace, marriage and parenting—ever more seriously ignorant and confused. Finally, having stumbled from one happenstance expediency to another, we enter into death even more unready—and far more unwilling.

In reading this clear and well developed guide, we not only make some actual inner shifts in understanding the death process—we find the insights an excellent, direct and compelling tool for use in actual life itself. Whether our life lies largely ahead of us, or largely behind, we will be the richer for our having learned something of that which the ancient Tibetans knew, made understandable and applicable to the modern Western world around us.

These teachings are presented within our own direct and familiar Judaic-Christian frames of reference and add to them immeasurably. As such, this study of the after-life transition periods is less alien than it might at first appear. And that, of course, displays the skill, scholarship and understanding of Mr. Grosz. May these pages enrich your own understanding and so your life. For the best preparation for death is, of course, a fully lived life—a life of commitment and purpose. Life and death are the perfect complementaries of each other, so learning well the one, enhances and prepares for the other. May you enter into both better prepared, mindful, responsible—and, why not, eager to explore the realms awaiting.

Joseph Chilton Pearce
Author of *The Crack in the Cosmic Egg,*
Magical Child, Magical Child Matures

1

I hear you are dying

Dear friend,

I hear you are dying and I'd like you to understand what is about to happen.

First of all, you must know that you are not alone. We are all dying. Flowers die when the season turns cold. Buildings die when earthquakes topple them. Cities die when fire guts them. Earth will die when the sun stops shining. People die when their bodies no longer work.

Death is a natural thing. The moment you are born you set yourself up to die. Therefore, if you don't want to die, don't get born. That's just the way it goes, for once you are born you must accept the fact that death goes hand in hand with birth, like it or not. My friend Peter used to joke that death is nature's way of getting you to slow down.

I often start my lectures on death and conscious-ness that exists beyond it by asking if there is anybody in the room who does not intend to die. Should I ever find such a person, I will sit down and let him or her talk. Clearly, this person will know much more than I do, and I will want to learn from him. So far, however, the only people who have raised their hands have ad-mitted they were joking when I invited them onto the podium to tell us how they plan to avoid dying.

Yet even though death is inevitable, it is merely a physical thing, and so it only affects things that are physical. My body is a physical thing and one day it will die. Your body is a physical thing, and one day, too, will die. That is what happens to physical things. It is never a question of if, with physical things; it is only a question of when.

But life is more than a physical thing. What power in the heart of a seed can make it grow into a tree? Do you need money or fame or power or looks to be alive? Is a person less human if she is old and feeble? Where is love really hidden? Can anything truly buy happiness if it is not already inside you? Aren't you always you?

There are no physical answers to these questions, though they have existed within each of us since humanity first walked on this planet, just as we have existed within the physical body ever since the planet was ready to receive us. For these are the questions of fools and children, philosophers and lovers. These are the questions of life.

The greatest teachers throughout the history of the world have said it is so. They have affirmed that life is found within, that life is more than death. They could not prove what they knew scientifically, for proof, like death, is physical and the life which they found within transcends the physical world and physical proof. Yet they spoke from the heart and had no reason to lie.

You are about to find what they found. You are about to experience the fact that life exists beyond the death of the physical body.

Life beyond death is different from life before death. As a result the ways of living, moving, and communicating which you have learned and adapted to during your stay on Earth will not necessarily apply in the realm of your new existence. You will be like a new-born babe when the life force leaves your body—as exposed to the

2

reality of that other world as is an infant newly born into this one. Future letters will discuss those differences so you may be prepared for them at the time you need to know.

The information here is not new. It is twelve hundred years old in the revelations of Padma Sambhava, founder of Tibetan lamaism; two thousand years old in the teachings of Jesus of Nazareth; and twenty-six hundred years old in those of Gutama, the Buddha. It is thirty-five hundred years old in the words received by Moses, and as old as humanity itself in the techniques of yoga, which permit the individual to go inside his very being to find that part of himself that lives forever.

But even though what is contained herein is ancient, as all eternal truth, it is only within our lifetime that this widely scattered knowledge has come together and been made available to the searching Western mind. And further, it is only within this same time frame that modern medical science has been able to resuscitate patients from the ranks of the clinically dead—patients who have reported the exact experiences which the ancient texts predicted. Think of it! *We are the first generation in the history of the world to have all of these forces come together for our knowledge and our use.* We would be fools not to use this knowledge.

The information given here has not yet been incorporated into the traditional Western religions as we know them today. Yet within one generation what is contained in these letters will be common knowledge and the subject of open discussion in the most conservative and orthodox of churches. Meanwhile these findings are being accepted by an ever-growing number of individuals of all faiths, who have found that they do not conflict with their previous beliefs, but augment them.

Life beyond death exists in one form or another for

all people, no matter what they believe. Open your mind without prejudice to some very interesting, very exciting ideas, and there will come a day when you will see for yourself. May these words help you when that day comes.

Peace and love

2
Fear need not be

Dear friend,

Fear is the strongest reason why people cannot face death. They have no idea what to expect and so they are terrified. It is human nature to fear what we do not know, and we are very human.

When you are young there is less fear than when you are old. When you are healthy, there is less fear than when you are sick. If you let it, fear can even put up a barricade to your search for the very answer to what it is you fear.

It is interesting that fear of death has not always been a part of the human attitude towards dying. Humanity in its earliest development was much more in tune with the natural rhythms of life and death than modern "civilized" people are today. They saw the life of day and the death of night, the life of summer and the death of winter, not just as annoyances which could be overcome with electric lighting and central heating, but as natural cycles which affect everything that is. They saw the sun die at night and be reborn at morning, Earth die in winter and be reborn in the spring, and life sprout from the ground where the corpses of last year's plants had fallen. They may not have understood how it worked, but they knew intuitively that it did.

As people who lived close to nature, they knew that

death is a natural thing, and because they knew that, they did not fear it. They saw new human life as the rebirth of the soul of a beloved ancestor, that the ancestor had not been lost when he died, but had merely worn out his old body and remained alive in the spirit while he waited to come back again in another form. And if ancestors continued to live in spirit, so would they. They may have tried to avoid pain as we all do, they may have grieved for the missing touch of a loved one as we all do, but they did not fear death, per se. There was nothing to fear.

Throughout the world, even up to the present time, pockets of unspoiled cultures continue to respect and accept death as a normal, natural part of the cyclical process. Western society, however, has set its mind to understanding and taming nature rather than accepting it for what it is. Although this has led to a greater and greater cornucopia of creature comforts, it has gotten us to the point where we no longer accept anything which we cannot understand.

In Europe, even up to the thirteenth century, death was recognized for the natural event it is, and as a result was easily accepted. Literature of that period abounds with accounts of a king or a knight feeling death coming on and taking to his bed, calling in his family and friends, settling his wordly affairs, saying the proper prayers, and easing back into the pillows to die in peace.

There was a dignity in dying, even though it took place without great fanfare or formal ceremony. The priest would be there, but only to perform the rituals; except for the Last Rites of the Church, the dying person was the one who set the pace and decided what would happen next. Family and friends came to say goodbye, and old disputes were settled, lest they get in the way of whatever the dying person expected to face on the other side.

Most importantly, the youngest of children and grand-children were always called in for one last visit. Not only did this help to create a sense of completion and fulfill-ment for the dying person, surrounded as he or she was by loved ones, but it exposed those youngsters at an early age to death, and taught them that death, though mys-terious, is natural. Contrast this with today's attitude, where children are kept far from both the scene and the truth because they are "too young to know." Thus, we create in the next generation the very fear we wish to avoid.

Over the next five hundred years numerous changes took place in how we view death. Religious emphasis broadened from a single judgment of all souls at the end of the world to judgment for each individual soul at the moment of death. At the same time, artists began por-traying, not spiritually uplifting scenes of souls enter-ing a new world, but physically graphic scenes of the decomposition of the body. These were both factors which appealed to the emotion of fear.

Little by little, death became a "thing" external to the individual, an evil to be avoided at all costs. By the nineteenth century, last wills and testaments had been turned into legal statements rather than spiritual ones and dying was no longer a natural event to be experi-enced in an aware, relaxed state. The dying person was no longer in control of what was happening. Religious experts were placed in charge of the rituals designed to protect the soul, while legal counselors were given do-minion over the documents dealing with the body and its possessions. It is only natural that fear should exist in such a situation, with so much being done "for you" while you have little or no control over what is going on.

Today in the West, with the exception of the hospice program, this situation has reached an extreme. For the majority of us, death no longer even occurs at home in familiar, comfortable surroundings. Decisions are not made by the dying person or even by the family, who most often are kept far away from what is happening. Instead, they are made by doctors who view death as a medical failure rather than as a natural occurrence which cannot be avoided. Patients are drugged and anesthetized and in many cases not told the facts, if they are even conscious. They are attached to monstrous electronic contraptions through which their very life force becomes only an input on a readout dial. Death is fought tooth and nail, with the focus placed not on the person who is dying, but on the attending physician and the latest technological breakthroughs. We've come a long way since the days of death with dignity . . . in the wrong direction.

Peace and love

3
Meditation techniques

Dear friend,

It is very important that death be faced in as peaceful and relaxed a state as possible. As you pass through the stages from life to death, much will be happening both to you and around you, and there will be decisions and choices for you to make which will determine where your consciousness heads and what happens next. If you make those decisions motivated by fear, you could end up being led into situations you would not choose to experience, as you shall see later on. However, if you are aware yet unafraid, alert yet at ease, you will recognize the signposts as they occur and thus know what is coming next. Indeed, if you take the teachings of these letters to heart, and learn how to produce and retain a feeling of inner peace, death can lead you to a state of unbounded bliss and happiness, a state that is the ultimate goal of all sentient beings.

And so I would like you to prepare for that event by putting yourself into a state of peace each day before reading these letters. Just as the astronauts practiced their moon landings over and over on Earth so they would be prepared and at ease when the time came for the real thing, I would like for you to do the same. An additional benefit of such practice is that when you are in that state of peace, you will be more open to receive the knowledge and feelings, the insights and understandings of those masters throughout the ages who have looked upon death not with fear and foreboding, but with awe and wonder. And though their teachings can do nothing to add one solitary moment to the length of your stay on this planet, they can do wonders to help you make the most of both the remaining days you have here and those which exist beyond.

The technique which we will use to generate that sense of serenity is known as *meditation,* a word which has been much misunderstood here in the West until very recently. To our knowledge, meditation was first practiced over five thousand years ago by the Aryans, an advanced race of people found in northern India who also developed mathematical principles and medical techniques so effective that they are still in use today. The Aryans taught meditation as a scientific tool to be used by the individual to reach and understand the inner self, the true being of each and every one of us, and the part of us that outlives the death of the body. They called this science yoga, which means "union," the union between the inner and the outer worlds.

You see, we are tied into the outer world by our five senses. Indeed, sights and sounds, smells, tastes, and sensations of feeling are constantly bombarding us, forming all of our connectors to the world in which we live and allowing us to be a part of it. Without these inputs we would have no way of relating to life around us. However, in addition to the physical world with which we are so familiar, we are also part of another whole realm of creation which exists on a nonphysical level. This is the inner world, and it is the one in which our senses don't work.

In fact, this inner world is so subtle and so delicate that any "noise" from the external world can block our attempt to find it. These days our external world is far too loud. Hence, the ever-growing belief in our high tech, high stimulus society that there is no inner world, no soul, nothing beyond the physical and the materialistic domains. However, over the centuries meditation has provided us with a systematic method of stilling the outer world so the inner one can be found. Even today meditation skills allow an individual to experience the inner level of consciousness which exists within each of us. And its beauty is that it can be used with any religion or belief system you wish.

The goal of the first phase of meditation is *quieting*, and you start, very simply, by turning off all radios and TVs and taking the phone off the hook. The idea is to close out the outside world and find the world within you, so shutting down the machines is a good place to begin. Get as comfortable as possible, either sitting up or lying down. There's no need to cross your legs or get in any fancy position. Let your arms and hands relax on your lap or on the bed, and close your eyes.

Breathe in and out taking slow deep breaths, but don't force anything. It's all got to be easy and natural. Focus your attention on the tip of your nose, the space between your nostrils, and feel the air coming in and going out. The breath is a good place to start your meditation because it is the connecting link between the world outside and the world inside. Outside air comes in, inside air goes out. Feel the cool air coming in. Feel the warm air going out. Keep your attention fixed on the end of your nose, and soon you will notice that your breathing has become slower and deeper, quieter and smoother, without your even trying. Feel peace and well-being enter your body with each inhalation. Feel tension and fear leave your body with each exhalation. With each breath feel yourself becoming more calm, more at peace. It is that simple.

At first you may be distracted by all sorts of thoughts

and lose concentration on your breathing. You'll think you're not doing it right and get discouraged. Well, that happens to everybody, so don't let it bother you. When you realize your mind has wandered, don't get mad, just say "oh," and go back to thinking about your breathing. Feel the cool air going up into your sinuses and imagine that it is breaking down all the tensions you have inside. Visualize those tensions and fears leaving your body along with the air you exhale. It's important not to try to force unwanted thoughts out of your mind. Forcing anything just causes tension, and tension is exactly what we're trying to remove. Just refocus and start again. There's no hurry.

Peace and love

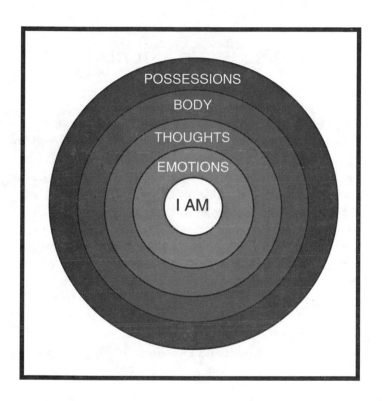

You are a complex being composed of numerous layers of individual presence and personality. All play a part in who you are and how you view yourself in your earthly existence in the physical world.

4
The undiscover'd country

Dear friend,

Many people run away from their fear of death by hiding in the world of money and material goods. They studiously avoid conscious thought of death by living a fever-pitched life while smothering themselves with the current fashions, latest fads, and highest priced electronic gadgets. If they consider death at all, it is only in the third person, something that can never happen to themselves because they are much too busy to take any time off. The motto of those who play this game is most clearly stated by the poster currently in circulation showing the Ultimate Consumer standing in front of his mansion, leaning on his Rolls Royce, surrounded by his sailboats, planes, and assorted belongings, all piled high around him. "The one who dies with the most toys," says the caption, "wins."

Even those whose lives are not driven by greed and the desire for acquisition find themselves caught up in the rush and the pressures of the material world. Old debts require constant work to be repaid, while new debts and obligations continue to accumulate. "I've got no time to think about death, it's tough enough keeping up with life." Thus they, too, insulate themselves from facing the question of what happens next. Meanwhile, that which is not faced can become a fear as its inevitability becomes more apparent.

The whole pace of modern life leads us to avoid confronting the basic issue of our ultimate future. Bombarded by external stimuli of the highest order, we accept the ease and luxury which our technology has to offer, even though each new state-of-the-art development leads us farther and farther away from our source, and places even more layers between us and nature, of which we are a part. We have separated ourselves from the natural cycles of life and now live, work, play, shop, and travel in hermetically sealed, temperature-controlled, constantly illuminated environments far removed from the natural world that surrounds them.

Technology has done wonders and created products which would appear as miracles to the eyes of earlier peoples. But we have put all our faith in technology without recognizing that such advances must fall within the realm of the natural laws which have existed since life on the planet first began. Death is one of these laws.

There is no way death can be averted for any living creature on the planet, even though every now and then it appears that the ultimate question can be pushed aside for a time. Some experts would have us believe that we can beat death, that we can take special drugs, undergo exotic treatments, exchange worn-out body parts for new ones, get hooked up to expensive machinery, and one way or another keep pushing death out farther into the distance until it finally gives up and moves on to someone else. Yes, modern medicine has developed procedures which serve to delay death, but make it disappear? Never! In the long run, as we have already noted, it is a natural law of the physical world that what goes up must come down, what lives must die, much as we might like to believe otherwise.

However, simply noting that all living beings must die at one point or another is not necessarily going to provide any solace, guidance, or direction for the individual whose death is clearly visible on the horizon. Intellectually we know that all living things die, but we each face death on our own. At least that's how it's been up till now!

It's fascinating. Modern medicine, the very science that has been trying to stave off death, has turned out to be the key to open the door and allow us to more fully understand it—like Columbus and his crew trying to reach India by sailing west and landing in America instead. It's not what they had in mind, but that's what happened, and the world hasn't been the same since.

You see, our views on death have been shaped by the fact that in the past when someone died, that was it. There was no way of knowing, at least for those people left alive, what the person who had passed over was experiencing, if indeed he was experiencing anything at all! As usual, Shakespeare said it best when he had Hamlet describe death as "that undiscover'd country from whose bourne no traveller returns." From the beginning of time up to the present, this has been true. No one, not even the great Houdini, was able to come back from beyond the veil and tell us what he saw.

But, thanks to modern medicine, we now have people who have been resuscitated from death and who have returned to tell us what it is like "on the other side." In fact, as of the middle of 1987, over eight million people in North America alone have come back to describe death return experiences. That includes a lot of doctors, nurses, and other scientifically trained professionals who wouldn't have believed a word of it had it not happened to them personally.

Now, you might be thinking: "Those people really weren't dead. The very fact that they came back to talk

16

about it is proof that they weren't dead. Dead is forever." Well, not any more, because these individuals were actually declared dead by the very practitioners of medicine who later brought them "back to life" with their modern miracles. In other words, they had passed the test of what the doctors defined as clinically dead, and only then were reanimated on this side of the veil. Were they dead or weren't they? It depends on how their doctors define death. You see, what we have here is not so much a question of what really happened as a question of semantics and what the doctors want to say happened. I'll explain what I mean by that in the next letter.

Peace and love

5

The traveler returns

Dear friend,

I'm sure that the first time artificial respiration was used to revive a drowning victim, it was considered a miracle. Word must have spread like wildfire throughout the community that someone had been brought back from the dead. Of course people would think so; no one had ever recovered from not breathing before!

But it doesn't matter whether the medical profession did not wish to lay claim to raising the dead, or whether pressure to do so was put on them in one form or another. What followed was simply that the definition of what it took to be dead changed. From that point on, not breathing didn't count. Your heart had to stop beating.

You know what happened next. We figured out ways to jump start the heart, so that definition of death became passé as well, and we went on to tracking brain waves. Well, progress being what it is, the cessation of brain activity is no longer a barrier to resuscitation either, so the medical profession (and the legal profession, I might add) are once again in a fog as to how to define this most basic element of life—death.

Meanwhile, one thing is perfectly clear. As modern science is continuing its advances in reanimating the body after longer and longer periods of death, the death return experiences which people are reporting have become more and more vivid and more and more common. This fact has not escaped the observation of the medical profession itself.

In fact, one of the very first books on the subject was written back in 1975 by a physician, Dr. Raymond A. Moody, Jr., and was entitled *Life After Life*. Its message is simple. Dr. Moody, a medical doctor, had encountered a number of people who had been resuscitated after having been declared clinically dead. These people all reported having had conscious experiences during this period, and Dr. Moody found their tales most interesting and challenging to the scientific beliefs then current.

What made these reports different from other accounts of life after death was the fact that the individuals involved represented a wide, eclectic spectrum. They differed from each other in age, sex, profession, location, upbringing, race, religion, and in the nature of the physical event that had brought them beyond death and back. Yet even though they were unacquainted with each other and with each other's stories, their descriptions were surprisingly similar! It could not be merely coincidental.

Of course, it might have been possible that these accounts had been made up by the individuals involved for the sole purpose of getting attention and having their stories written up in the newspaper. However, logic tells us no. Up to that point in time people who told of living outside the body were not honored and esteemed by Western society as they are in the East. If anything, they were put down, ridiculed as being crazy, accused of having hallucinations, or, at the very least, called mentally unstable. People who shared these highly personal experiences were laughed at and made fun of and set up as objects of public censure. There was nothing to gain and no possible reason for these stories to be fabricated. Clearly, from the point of view of the person involved, the experiences had been absolutely real.

Also, if the stories recounted by the various victims had been pure fantasy one could assume a wide variety of scenarios. Yet this was not the case. All the accounts displayed the same elements and made virtually the same observations. This was very interesting, since one of the things science considers proof of an experiment is its reproducibility; the same results should be obtained by anyone who tries the experiment. In this case, reproducibility was occurring spontaneously.

Of course, there was still the possibility that the whole book was a work of fiction. Could Dr. Moody have been putting us on, if indeed there was a Dr. Moody after all? Well, needless to say, there is a real Dr. Raymond A. Moody, Jr., and he risked his entire medical reputation by what he wrote. Yet he was circumspect; he did not allow himself to draw final conclusions which might be considered to go one tiny step beyond what could be deduced directly from the reports of the many patients interviewed. There is no question that Dr. Moody had not fabricated but had reported honestly and truthfully what real individuals had told him. As a result, a new door had been opened in understanding life's greatest mystery.

And now comes the kicker, the most exciting and amazing part of the puzzle. All those stories of life beyond death, those firsthand accounts of existence beyond the body which paralleled each other and led to the scientific community's rethinking of the very basis of life and reality, have something else in common as well. The vast majority of death return experiences describe with awe and wonderment scenes directly out of the *Bardo Thödol*, a mystic Tibetan book written twelve hundred years ago on the other side of the world! This is no coincidence. This is no fabrication. This is not the result of conspiracy or hallucination. This is a fact whose time has come! This is cold, hard, unemotional, scientific reality that agrees with ancient esoteric texts. Can you feel the importance of what has happened?

Now, for the very first time in the history of humanity, both intellect and intuition lead to the same inevitable conclusion—there is a separate consciousness which lives on beyond the death of the physical body! You will experience life after your body dies. It is so. Know it to be true. You will live!

Peace and love

6
The continuum of masters

Dear friend,

There is life after death. Not the slightest question about it should exist in your mind. Scientists may say it has not been proved. You can answer, "Your instruments are merely unable to detect it; nevertheless, it is true." Psychologists may say it is all in your mind. You can answer, "It is the mind that survives into the other world. Therefore we agree." Skeptics may say you only wish it to be so. You can answer, "I have wished it to be so and my wish has been granted."

Oh, there will continue to be "studies," as doubting researchers try to understand what is happening, try to rationalize their old beliefs in light of the new reality. They will continue to gather data, develop high-tech experiments, interview patients, and ask the same worn-out questions over and over. They will insist on denying that which they cannot see with the eye, hear with the ear, feel with the hand, smell with the nose, or taste with the tongue. But your consciousness, the part of you that continues to live beyond the death of the body, cannot be measured by gross instruments. As long as technicians continue to look for otherworld answers with the tools and senses of this world, they will never find what they are seeking. This is unfortunate for them and a crime for those who believe them.

22

There will also be those who refuse to believe anything not specifically defined by the particular religious doctrine they follow. Here, too, a greater understanding must develop which overrides narrow definitions. For though the words of the masters are true for all ages, we must remember that those to whom they were preaching at the time were simple, unsophisticated folk who were thousands of years behind us in schooling and experience. They could not be expected to openly accept concepts and ideas which are matters of fact to us today. Learning builds on what comes before it, and though what was taught then may have been the truth, it was designed for the ears of those who were there to hear it. There were still more teachings that humanity was not yet ready to receive. Does not Jesus say, "I have yet many things to say unto you, but ye cannot bear them now"? (John 16:12) And is that not also the truth?

Also, the fact that a certain master speaks truth does not mean that other masters speak falsehoods. It is more likely that they each have their own lessons to teach and that a continuum of masters is building on what came before them, each one taking humanity farther along the path. Moses taught of one God, unseen yet all-powerful, unable to be pictured, unable to be named other than "I am that I am." Jesus felt that "I am" within and showed that God can walk on Earth clothed in a human body. Today we know that same "I am" lives in each one of us. Each teaching is true; each advances the truth. There are more new truths now which mankind is ready to receive.

The fact that other cultures have given us specific depictions of what life is like across the veil of death should not be a stumbling block to our acceptance of them. Different masters teach different things. You know they speak truth because they fit in with previous masters' truths. The *Nag Hammadi Library*, a collection of early Christian writings recently unearthed in Egypt after being buried for over sixteen hundred years, says it well. In a work entitled *The Apocalypse of Peter*, Christ shows Peter the afterworld and says, "These things, then, which you saw you shall present to those of another race who are not of this age." NHL (VII, 3) 83. Could these words have been proclaiming the future existence of the *Bardo Thödol*, the Tibetan book whose words are so meaningful for those in the West who face death today?

Please understand, my friend, it is not my purpose to discuss theology or to argue for any one person's belief versus anyone else's. There is enough of that going on in the world already, and it only tends to separate people, not bring them together. This book has been written for the same reason that the *Bardo Thödol* was penned twelve hundred years ago, not as an intellectual or esoteric curiosity, but as a practical self-study guide to life in the afterworld, the world which your spirit will face upon the death of your body.

This book is a synthesis of all that came before it. It affirms the eternal nature of the human soul, based not only on spiritual teachings from around the world and throughout time, but also on the modern scientific breakthroughs which have finally confirmed what the masters have been teaching all along. If your mind and heart are open to the unfolding of the New Age, the joy and bliss which these words will help you to experience will be greater than any treasure Earth has to offer.

If you are one who questions but does not know for sure, would like to see before believing, would like to accept but are not yet certain, let me suggest that doubt is as strong a springboard for belief as for disbelief. The same feelings that tell you that something may not be can also be viewed from the other side as if it were so.

The open door has two sides. Ask, "What if it is?" rather than, "What if it isn't?"

It is a fact that answers do not come to those who do not question. Just as diamonds do not fall into the grasp of those who stand at the entrance to the mine, similarly, spiritual truths do not unfold before the individual who will not delve inside. Open your mind and join it to your heart. Turn your doubts into questions. Use your intuitive powers to change your questions into belief. Then knowledge will turn your belief into faith. This work is not fiction. Read it, study it, practice it, and take it seriously. Soon you will know its true value.

Peace and love

7
Where do we go from here?

Dear friend,

As mentioned in the last letter, my purpose here is not just to present information for your intellectual curiosity. There are enough books around that do just that, and then refuse to come to any definite conclusion. These letters are different. They not only accept the after-death experience as the truth it is, they actually comprise a study guide intended to allow you, while still alive, to understand what it is you will experience after your body dies. As you will see, knowing this information in advance should prove quite useful both during and after the actual event.

This work is a road map intended to lead you safely through both the process of death and the world you will experience on the other side. As with any road map, this one shows both the nice neighborhoods and the not-so-nice neighborhoods, and can lead you anywhere you want to go. However, simply looking at a map does not cause you to arrive at one location or another. Your destination is strictly up to you. Some people live their lives motivated by fear, others by anger, others by greed, others by love. Each of these individuals will come to certain forks in the road, and each will choose to travel different paths. But your having studied the map beforehand at least gives you the option of knowing what lies ahead.

Since this material is new to Western thought, there will be some ideas and concepts presented which could initially prove confusing, and to minimize this I'd like to define a few terms. First, the word "death." Up to this point I've been adding the phrase "of your body." However, that in truth is the only death possible, and so from here on in you will know without my even saying it that "death" refers only to the flesh you've been carrying around all these years. If you still have any doubts or reservations, go back and reread the first six letters, or pore through some of the books listed in the Suggested Reading Guide at the end of this book. Or for the sake of this study just try to accept the premise that you will be conscious and aware after your death. Either way, progress can only be made by keeping an open mind. Best of all, practice the various meditation techniques and you will soon find out the truth firsthand.

The second word we need to define has to do with the part of you that does continue to live after death. Here there are several good terms in the language which we can use, such as "spirit," "soul," and "consciousness." They all mean just about the same thing, even though some people have prejudices towards one or another. I'll switch them depending on what feels good at the time; it will help make the writing more interesting. Besides, it really doesn't matter what we call it; the important thing is that it *is*.

Finally, we need a word for that place where your soul will emerge after death. It is, as you will see, neither a heaven nor a hell, but more like a way station with a number of interesting characteristics which you will pass through prior to moving on. There is no Western word in common usage that means quite the same, and so, since the Tibetans are the experts at exploring this realm, we shall import the Tibetan word "bardo." In Tibetan "bardo" means "the intermediate state," and it is very appropriate that we learn and use this term.

One more important bit of information, and then we're ready to describe what you should experience as you approach the moment of death and go beyond it. It may sound silly to have to say this, but you must not forget that you will no longer be operating with the constraints of a physical body. That's the part of you you're leaving behind, much like a snake shedding his skin. Now just stop and think about this for a moment.

On Earth, the world you're living in now, when you want to get from place to place you walk, or you drive, or you take a bus, or you swim, or you hop a plane, or you just plain hop. When you want to change the scenery, no matter where you want to go, you must move your body to the place where you want it to be. You may be thinking about a beautiful sunlit beach, but if you haven't booked an airline seat, you'll find when you look around that you're still right where you started. That beautiful beach may be in your mind, but you and your body are still at home, and there's still a blizzard outside.

In the bardo things are different. Without your body to constrict you, where you imagine you are is where you are! And if you think this sounds weird, you're right. But, stop to reflect for just an instant. Haven't there been times when you have been lost in a thought, been involved in some mental image that grabbed your attention so strongly that when someone nudged your arm, or the school bell rang, or the factory whistle blew, you had to take a second or two to realize where you were? Or how about dreams that seemed so real—until the alarm went off and you awoke? Well, in the bardo you don't "awaken" because there is no physical world to

28

awaken to. You already are awake in a world without physical bodies, a world where your very thoughts and feelings will move you from place to place in an instant. While this has its benefits, such as your being able to travel at will simply by changing your thoughts, it also has its drawbacks. How many of us actually control our thoughts? How many of us actually think only what we want to think? Often thoughts and emotions creep into our minds uninvited. We shudder, open our eyes, and are still in our easy chairs. But in the bardo such thoughts are the very means of motion. They could transport you farther and farther into undesirable neighborhoods. But forewarned is forearmed. That is what these letters are all about.

Peace and love

8
Meditation techniques

Dear friend,

Today's letter is going to teach some additional techniques of meditation which you can use in reaching the goal of finding that inner world and the spirit that resides there. Remember always that the reason for practicing meditation is twofold. First, it allows you to eliminate the fear and tension normally associated with death in our day and age. Thus, you will be able to face the natural transition in peace and with dignity, unafraid and totally aware of everything that is going on. Second, and even more importantly, meditation can put you in touch with your very soul, that part of you which survives and continues to live after its separation from the body. Knowing who you really are and being able to control your thoughts and emotions will be a key to the life you will experience beyond death.

Start by quieting yourself, as you have been doing with the breathing technique we have already discussed. Take some slow breaths and focus your attention on the cool air coming in and the warm air going out. Let peace and well-being enter you with each intake of air, while tension and fear leave with each outflow. By now you may have begun to feel a certain ease and relaxation which comes when you meditate, and that can't be all bad, in and of itself. You may also have found that meditating has allowed you to fall asleep easier, or at some point you may have had a flash feeling of something akin to dreaming, even though you know you're wide awake. All of these are signs that you're on the right track. If you haven't had these feelings yet, don't despair. Every time you meditate you make some progress. The results will become evident if you keep going.

I want to discuss *focusing,* which is simply the practice of putting something into your mind and aiming all your attention at it so that you are completely unaware of anything else that is going on. Another way of looking at it is to say that focusing is simply concentrating your mind totally on one particular thing so that there is no room for anything else to intrude. In effect, that is what you have already been doing with the breathing exercise. Other thoughts may have come up, but as soon as you recognized their presence, you just went back to studying your breathing. I have heard the process described as being similar to cleaning an inkwell, not by pouring out the ink, but by simply continuing to pour clean water into the well, thereby displacing the dirty liquid you want removed. In the same way, by attending only to your breathing, your other thoughts eventually dissolve, and your mind becomes one-pointed.

It is possible to meditate by focusing on anything you wish. I used to turn off the lights and stare at the flame of a candle set on the table in front of me. As I gazed, the light from the flame would build and build until the entire room seemed bright. I would lower my head and feel the candlelight reaching me in the center of my forehead, the space between the eyebrows known as the "Third Eye." Other thoughts would vanish, and I would feel myself becoming one with the flame, as pure and as clean as fire. I always emerged from these sessions refreshed and energized.

31

Of course, what works for me may or may not work for you, and a method which I use to shut out the noise of the outside world and the chatter going on inside my head may not be the one that you end up using. That's okay; some people focus on trees, or running water, or sky, or a statue, or a painting, or a beautiful picture in a book. It doesn't matter where you place your attention as long as you direct it somewhere. You'll wind up finding the image that feels right and comfortable for you and that's the most important thing.

Some people are more attuned to sound than to sight, and for such persons a *mantra* is the best way to create an internal focal point for meditation. This is another one of those words that we in the West have tended to relate strictly with Eastern spiritual practices. However, this should not be so, for a mantra is nothing more than a particular sound repeated over and over until everything else is gone but the associated images that go with that sound. The Catholic woman on her knees repeating the rosary is using a mantra. The Jewish man deep in prayer intoning the Sh'ma is using a mantra. Whatever you choose, whatever you keep repeating in your head, after a while makes all other sounds and thoughts disappear. You must be careful, however, for every mantra produces its own image and its own internal feeling. Those who have wanted to seize political power have long known this, and they recognize the value a short catchy phrase will have on the masses if it is repeated loudly enough and often enough. "We want war" chanted over and over will most definitely not produce the same feelings among the population as "We want peace."

Your internal mantra can also be a major factor in both how you view yourself and how you face the world. The words "yes I can," repeated over and over by an athlete straining to finish a race, a little train trying to get over the mountain, or a person looking to make the most out of the remaining days of his life, become a mantra of faith and energy, strength and power. "I am at peace" is a mantra which produces calmness and serenity, comfort and clarity of mind. My own favorite is "All This Is God." It reminds me that we are all one, and that if I still myself and listen to the voice inside, I will do the right thing even though I may not know why. It makes me feel good, it makes me feel peaceful. Try it with my blessings.

Focusing on an image or a mantra any time you feel nervous or tense or uptight or frightened will make you feel good inside and help you to overcome fear and find serenity. It will also help you to accept death for what it is. And that will help you to accept life for what it is, as well.

Peace and love

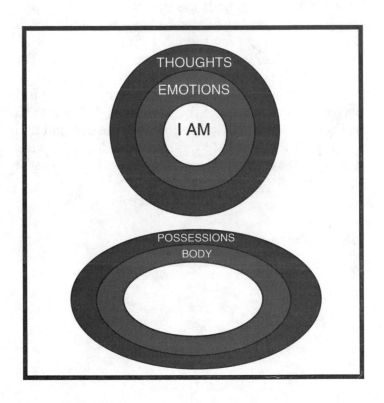

When you die, those layers which are of the physical world remain in the physical world. The rest of your presence and personality accompanies you into the bardo. You are still you. You just have fewer layers covering your absolute perfect core.

9
Looking back

Dear friend,

There is so much to share with you about what happens next—what it feels like to die; how to move by thought control; what places you might want to visit; what places you might want to avoid; what you will encounter and why—just to mention a few things. But first I'd like you to share the experiences we referred to before, of people who approached death, went beyond it, and came back to report what they saw. Take some time to feel what they felt. Later on when we do get into the actual teachings of the bardo, you will be able to relate what is said there to the actual experiences reported by people just like yourself—modern Westerners going through the most natural of human events, dying.

Let's set the scene. It could be in a hospital room where a middle-aged woman undergoing an abdominal operation suffers a cardiac arrest. Doctors and nurses pound on her chest and rush in the defibrillator, which they will use to electrically shock her heart in an attempt to restart it. Or perhaps it is on a city street where a forty-two-year-old jogger suddenly feels pain in his chest. He falls to the ground and is surrounded by curious onlookers. Someone runs down to the corner to tell the cop who is directing traffic. It could be during war, when a young soldier in the peak of physical condition is hit by gunfire or steps on a land mine. One moment he is alive and aware, the next moment he is in a different world. It could even be in a quiet bedroom where an old man notices with a detached sense of curiosity that the pain he has been living with for all these years is gone. In other words, it can happen wherever people live, while they are doing whatever people do, whenever it is that people die.

There are a number of different feelings that people have reported having had as they pass from one world to the other. And though not everyone experiences all of them, there is a lot of common ground. For one thing, (and this is universal) there is a lack of pain. The soldier does not feel his wounds; the pressure is gone from the jogger's chest; the patient on the operating table doesn't even sense the shock running through her body, though her body jumps high in the air as the electrical charge is applied. The explanation is simple, for at this point consciousness has separated from the body. Physical pain is clearly a function of the physical body, and without a body to receive and send sensory inputs, pain cannot exist. In fact, this lack of pain is often the first clue the subject has that something is happening. There is an overall feeling of peace, comfort, and well-being at this stage, though there can be some real confusion for the person who thought that only the physical world exists.

Individuals often observe with interest what is going on in the vicinity of their now lifeless physical form. The jogger may watch with rapt attention as the policeman attempts emergency mouth-to-mouth resuscitation. He may even wonder who that poor fellow on the ground is, and make a mental note of the coincidence that the man is wearing the same shorts and T-shirt that he himself had put on that morning. The soldier may see the enemy scout creep through the bushes, and though he tries to reach for his rifle, he cannot get his arms to move.

He can do nothing but watch helplessly as the boots are removed from his immobile body.

At some point early on, the newly deceased soul will come to the realization that these observations are not occurring from the familiar vantage point within the body. There is a strange and unusual detachment, a feeling of separation. The person is not seeing in the normal fashion, with the eyes from within the head. Most people feel like they are floating above what is happening, looking down from high in the air as others scurry around below. The hospital patient watches from the ceiling as the doctors try to reanimate her body. The old man hovers above his bed as his daughter and son-in-law hold on to each other and weep.

And one can hear as well as see. The woman in the hospital room knows everything being said. If she hasn't figured it out already, the first inkling of her death may come from hearing the doctor say, "We've lost her." The soldier notes helicopters coming to evacuate the bodies; the jogger hears the ambulance racing towards the crowd on the sidewalk. But through it all—though there may be frantic movement and activity going on all around and a sense of all-important purpose for those participating in the activities—for the subject himself, out of pain and viewing the scene from his detached vantage point, all is quiet, all is at peace.

There may be confusion; the person might wonder what tricks his mind is playing. The body below is lifeless, but he is here and very much alive. He seems to be outside of and separate from his body, and he doesn't know what is going on. He wants to communicate to others, to tell them where he is, to tell them he's all right but no one hears. The old man reaches for his children to let them know that he is fine, that the pain is gone, but he cannot get through to them.

Then eventually there dawns the realization that this

must be what is known as death. The jogger sees the face of the man on the ground; the patient watches as the doctors unplug the defibrillator; the soldier's body is placed in a bag; the old man's eyelids are closed and kissed.

For a number of individuals, this is where the other-world journey ends. With a sudden "swoosh" they are pulled back into their bodies. "Medic!," yells the helicopter pilot as he sees a finger move. "We've got a beat," the nurse staring at a TV tube calls out. But not all come back here. Some stop looking out at the world they've come from and start observing the world they're in.

Peace and love

10
Looking around

Dear friend,

The most common factor in the reports of people who have had a death return experience is that they just can't find the words to describe what they have encountered. Isn't that amazing! This is the most phenomenal situation they have ever found themselves in, the most unique experience they have ever undergone, and they can't even find the right words to express it!

When you stop to think about it, however, it's actually not that strange at all. Language is built up by a tacit agreement to utilize a specific sound to indicate a specific meaning. That's what turns sounds into words. Words, in turn, are only of value if they mean the same thing to the person hearing them as they do to the person saying them. If they don't, it's like an Englishman trying to give directions to someone who only speaks Chinese. They'd probably end up using sign language and drawing pictures, communicating without words.

But even that type of communication is still far easier than what is faced by someone coming back from death and trying to tell what she saw to one who hasn't been there. The listener cannot possibly comprehend the images being conveyed because absolutely nothing like it has ever even crossed his mind; he has no frame of reference at all. It's the frustration of trying to explain the color red to a blind person, or describing the flavor vanilla to one who has never tasted ice cream. You know what you mean; you can see it, you can taste it, you can feel it; but how in the world do you get it across to someone who hasn't been there and doesn't even know where to look? There are simply no words which might not unintentionally mislead.

That's the problem in a nutshell. That's why it sounds as if those returning from death are tongue-tied, not because they don't know what happened with a remarkable clarity and sureness, but because our language just isn't big enough. What they have gone through over there just does not take place over here, and there are truly no words yet in our language to describe it. In the future, as more and more people slip back and forth across the boundary, the words will appear and become part of our common usage. However, till that time, we'll just have to do the best we can, even though our Earth-bound vocabulary falls so far short of what we are trying to describe. Someday the light will dawn and you'll feel it for yourself. "Oh," you'll say, "so that's what he meant."

It's not that easy for most people to tear themselves away from the physical world they have gotten so used to. But for those who do, who have not already been pulled back into their bodies and who choose to examine their new surroundings, they find themselves in a space which appears to be dark, black, and completely void. It is not a hard, solid black but gives off a softer feeling, more of a velvet black. There is an awareness of space and depth, although there is nothing here that could be defined as size or dimension. You can see within this darkness, not with your eyes, but with more of a comprehending, a knowing, a feeling of what is there. Along with the dark, there is an equally intense silence, not so much the silence of nothingness as a silence of all sound compressed into silence. As with sight, hearing is perfectly clear, although it is independent of the ears. Actually, it's not so much hearing as a feeling of sound. This is where words fall short; it is simply easier to call it hearing.

There is also often an understanding that one is dead, and an all-encompassing feeling of peace and tranquility, contentment and love. Those who have returned from the bardo say that although they felt disconnected and separated from their bodies, they had no regrets. It was as if in shedding the physical, an even greater world of knowledge and understanding had been unveiled to them, which made the body seem unimportant and a limiting factor in the overall scheme of things. The only regrets which people have mentioned feeling were not for the loss of their own physical lives, but for what would happen to those left behind, the spouse or child who would now be on his or her own.

Many people report having felt as if they still had a body, though not like the one they were used to. This new body has been described as being transparent and filmy, light and airy, sometimes shapeless, sometimes spherical, sometimes almost like a shadow of the one they left behind. What is most exciting for people with physical impairments is the fact that these new bodies seem to be whole, complete, and in perfect working order. There do not appear to be any blind or deaf, halt or lame persons across the veil of death. But no matter what the new body looks like, it feels as if it has no bodily weight. And rather than walking, people report a floating sensation. Movement is not done consciously; it is more like simply being transported to where you want to be.

Those who have died also experience a unique sense of timelessness, as if time doesn't matter, as if it doesn't even exist. Along with this comes an overpowering, heightened awareness of the present, a tuning in to everything that is occurring at the moment, although the individual may not understand or be able to explain it. How strange that people who have lived their whole lives on Earth by the clock and the calendar, scheduling and filling up every moment of the day from the morning alarm to the eleven o'clock news, upon returning, find it impossible to say how long their experience on the other side had been. More importantly, they don't even seem to care.

But strange as this all may appear, as wild and imaginative as this all may seem, everyone who enters the bardo and returns swears that it is as real as anything they have ever experienced on Earth!

Peace and love

11
Looking ahead

Dear friend,

Can you begin to understand what has happened to these people who have had death return experiences? Can you sense the wonder and amazement which enfold them upon their return to life from a world and an environment completely different from anything they had ever experienced before; a world which they never, ever expected to find; a world which they never even suspected existed? To be alive, to be aware, to see, to feel, to hear, to be a person as much as ever, yet not to have a body, no flesh and blood, no skin and bones. This is beautiful, exciting and beautiful.

For a number of persons who have traveled this far in the bardo, the journey ends. They experience separation from their bodies and the end of pain. They hear the earthly sounds and see the earthly sights while hovering above their physical remains. They observe the void, listen to the silence, and feel the separation from time, and the deep peace and tranquility which the new environment provides. Against their very will sometimes they are then pulled back into their bodies, their consciousness trapped once again inside their heads, their movements limited once again to the span and gait of their arms and legs. Yet, as exciting and incredible as the adventures of these people have been, others have gone even farther.

As many individuals begin to look around their new environment, they notice a point of light at what appears to be the end of a long tunnel. Pushed along by unseen winds or pulled by the lure of the illumination (it is hard to tell which), they are propelled through that tunnel and burst into a space of brilliant light, more clear, more blinding, than any they have ever seen before. It is a beautiful light, a living light, a light that fills their entire consciousness and being. And the light itself has a consciousness of absolute peace, absolute love, absolute perfection, which makes itself known to the individual soul. I have personally experienced this light, and can tell you with all my heart that at that moment, that most extraordinary moment, I knew I was in the presence of Oneness, the Source of all things, the Universal Consciousness, the Power that people call God. And I am not the only one who has been so blessed.

Many have passed through the tunnel, and to all who have the meeting with the light is the most indescribable part of an indescribable journey. Its memory can never be erased. Still others have felt a presence, or seen relatives or friends who had died earlier coming joyfully to greet them, holding out their arms, welcoming them to their new home. Some have felt the presence of Jesus Christ, or of angels and celestial beings shining in a beautiful translucent radiance, who call them with their arms outstretched and comfort them, removing their worries and fears, sending them love and peace. Some have seen beautiful scenery and vistas: rolling hills, lush fertile valleys, or magnificent cities corresponding to their individual ideas of what heaven would be. Each version is different, but each one is real.

Eventually, in all these cases, something has occurred to bring the person back to the physical world. She may see a line of trees or a river or a doorway and know that crossing it will sever her connection with Earth forever. She may experience just the slightest moment of hesitation, and she's back. Or she may want to stay but is told to return, that her life is not yet finished; and with a sudden rush she is drawn into the body again. Often this brings regret, for here there is pain and anxiety; there, pure peace.

Oh, those who have not been there may try to say from their perspectives of limited knowledge that the very fact we came back proves that we hadn't died. But we know better. Death is not a sudden thing, an on-off that either is or isn't, even though the machines that measure it are. Death is a process with a number of stages most of which exist outside of the body. Let scientists learn to keep the body intact for greater periods of time while there's no one inside, and they will receive longer, even more detailed reports of what it is like on the other side.

No one who has ever had a death return experience ever forgets it, for there is no longer any question of whether or not there is life after death. One has actual and absolute knowledge that there is. And so it cannot help but be a life-transforming experience which changes every fiber in a person's being. The biggest question of all has been answered.

Think of it, my friend. You will continue to be after death, for you are not the body in which you have been living for these past few years. You are a consciousness, a spirit, a soul that exists independently of the body which it inhabits for an ever-so-short period of time. How does it work? What is it that permits you to see without eyes, to hear without ears, to feel without flesh? How can a light be alive? Oh, how hard it is to explain these things in words. Yes, these are interesting questions, but must you have the answers to everything before you can accept their existence? Does it really matter how everything works, as long as you know that it does?

You will live beyond death. Know that to be true regardless of your religious beliefs or how you have lived your life. If you get nothing more from these writings than that, they will have been of value to you. But there is more, and if you can learn from the experiences of others, if you have the ears to hear, if you can see that it makes no sense to train for a hundred-yard dash when you are entered in a marathon, then you have truly understood.

Peace and love

12
The out-of-body experience

Dear friend,

The last three letters have summarized the visions and feelings recounted by the ever-growing number of persons who have gone through death return experiences. Although some individuals traveled farther into the bardo than others, all their accounts bear a striking similarity to one another, particularly in the energies that were generated during the trip and in the new sense of understanding, peace, and purpose one carries back to Earth.

Meanwhile, as the number of people having these experiences continues to increase, an interesting parallel is taking place which produces similar effects and can shed some light on what is actually occurring. This phenomenon is known by a number of terms including "out-of-body experience" and "astral projection," and is characterized by the sudden disconcerting jolt of finding one's mind separated from one's body. The sensation is more than that of just drifting off into a daydream, and can be quite unnerving the first time it happens. As with death return experiences, people will see their bodies from the outside as if they belonged to a completely different, completely separate individual. It may be a sudden thing lasting only a second or two, or it may be much longer, involving the actual floating of consciousness to a place where the body is no longer even visible. In either case, there is no question that the person is outside of the body, especially when one is hovering below the ceiling or drifting over a grove of trees.

Actually, stories of this nature are nothing new, having been reported by both saints and laymen throughout recorded history. Indeed, the author of The Book of Revelation as well as a number of Old Testament prophets attest to being "in the spirit" while making prophesies and receiving visions. In the West, through the middle ages such experiences were attributed to witchcraft or considered the "work of the devil," and thus tended to be suppressed by those who did not wish to end their days as martyrs. The rise of the scientific age in the seventeenth and eighteenth centuries further added to the belief that anything that could not be proved with cold, hard mathematical facts simply could not be. From that time on till recently, astral projection was practiced secretly, save for the work of the transcendental poets and psychics such as Edgar Cayce, whose contributions were tolerated but not accepted by mainstream thinking.

That has changed. Back in 1971, Robert Monroe, a Virginia businessman, published a work entitled *Journeys Out of the Body,* in which he discussed his first-hand experiences and experiments with the separation of body and mind. While unsure at first of what was happening to him during his unsolicited journeys, he nevertheless accepted them as real and didn't fear them, and he strove both to test what was occurring and to control it. As was the case with Moody's, this book also opened the door to further understanding. Suddenly, people who had had such experiences began surfacing.

It was in 1977 that I heard my first personal account when a friend opened up to tell me of his out-of-body experience. He had been in the hospital in New York

City recuperating from surgery and had heard that the temperature would be dropping below zero. That night as he slept, he felt himself leave the bed and travel to his home upstate, where he went into the basement to check on the status of the oil burner. Finding it turned off, he then went to his daughter's bedroom and "whispered" to her to turn on the furnace. The following morning, as he was pondering what had happened, his daughter called and told him how he didn't have to worry how she and her mom were getting on in his absence. As an example, she told of getting up in the middle of the night and going downstairs to turn on the oil burner, something she had never done before. All this was shared with me in confidence; he didn't want it getting around the office.

A lot has happened since then, with the subject receiving widespread interest and attention, thanks in part to public figures sharing their experiences, as Shirley MacLaine has done in *Out On a Limb*. All this tends to show that out-of-body experiences are as real as death return experiences, and can happen to anybody without the need for alcohol, drugs, marijuana, or LSD.

In reality, both events are manifestations of the very same truth, and lead to the very same conclusion: namely, that the soul is independent of the body and can exist on its own. Both trips produce the same loss of physical feeling; both produce the same lucid awareness; both produce the same alteration of consciousness which yields a certainty of the existence of a dimension of life which transcends gross physical reality. The fact that those who have been out-of-body do not report the same singularity of direction as those who have had death returns only indicates that as long as the body is healthy, the nonphysical traveler is free to go anywhere her heart desires. When she wants to return home, her body is there, empty and waiting, attached to her soul (so some

49

report) by an infinitely flexible and extendable silver or golden cord.

The death-return traveler, on the other hand, has been forcibly severed from that physical body and the soul is now being pulled by an even subtler connecting cord, one that leads to the basic core of life itself. It is only by the intrusion of an outside force and effort that the body is resuscitated and once again made habitable for the soul. That is the only difference between the two journeys, and it is an Earthly one. On the larger scale they are the same and feel the same, no matter what they are called. Thus the experienced out-of-body traveler will not be caught unaware when his body and soul separate at the moment of death. I am also certain that that is how the Tibetan lamas brought back their findings about the other side of death; findings which form the next portion of this book.

Peace and love

13
Meditation techniques

Dear friend,

By now you should be well on the path to becoming comfortable with meditation. Of course, it is impossible to predict how rapidly you are progressing because everyone is different, and there are so many subtle factors which can have an effect on the results. For example, if you have the ability to daydream, you will find it much easier to block out the surrounding sensory inputs than if you have never given way to inner flights of fancy. Also, if you still equate meditation with foreign religious practices, this could produce an unconscious blockage to success. Far better to understand that meditation is a systematic, nondenominational practice available for use by anyone who wishes to reach the Self inside.

It is also a fact that the sincere desire to reach this door to the inner world is the most important possible aid to finding it. That desire, you see, frees you from the tension and fear of the unknown which can block the acceptance of new and different experiences. You should have no such fear, for you know that you will be facing this inner world someday in any case. Meditation just gives you the opportunity to become acquainted with it in a controlled situation while your body still lives. Once you find this inner Self, your whole perspective on the life you have lived and the death you are facing will change. And I say this not just from my studies, but from personal experience. You have nothing to lose by practicing meditation, and you have an eternity to gain.

You see, it is one thing to *understand* what is happening through the use of intellect; it is another thing completely to *feel* what is happening through the use of instinct and intuition. These two are parts of you that point in the direction of your inner Self, the real you. They are also parts that survive death and need to be developed for your upcoming excursion through the bardo.

It has already been noted that during meditation you could have the feeling of just awakening from a dream, as if you had lost track of time. This is an indication that, for a split second at least, you had been focused inwardly away from the external senses, and this is good. It is only by the loss of our external orientation and focus that our inner orientation and focus can be developed, and that is the goal we are trying to achieve. Also, it is not uncommon for people who are just beginning to practice meditation to fall asleep while they're working on it. That's okay; it is a fine way to get a solid night's sleep, something we can all surely use. Falling asleep while meditating can also produce some very interesting, very vivid dreams. But dreaming and meditating are not the same, and the differences are important and worth noting.

In dreams you tend to identify completely with the image of yourself that you view on the inner screen of your mind. The philosopher Chuang Tzu once awoke from a dream and remarked, "I am a man who dreamed he was a butterfly; or," he added as an afterthought, "perhaps I am a butterfly who is now dreaming he is a man."

While you and I may not be as poetic as an ancient Chinese Taoist, we can both identify with the fact that in a dream everything seems real. If you are being chased by a large vicious-looking dog, you run. And if that dog gets closer, you panic and look for ways to escape. If you trip and fall and the dog bares his teeth and leaps for your throat—you wake up in a cold sweat feeling sort of silly. "Thank God," you mumble to yourself, "it was only a dream."

But the fact that you cannot physically be hurt by what happens in your dreams doesn't make them any less real while they are going on. Therapists are constantly visited by unfortunate individuals who are afraid to go to sleep because of the nightmares that await them. Tormented by their visions at night, and unable to forget during the day that such visions will return when they once again must give in to sleep, they live in constant tension and anxiety. How sad that must be, to fear the gentlest, most relaxing of nature's times.

Meditation, on the other hand, allows you to remain aware of the fact that you can control the image that is appearing on your inner screen. Thus, if in a meditative state you were to experience that same dog chasing you, you would be able to change the inner image as easily as you change a TV channel. You could mentally erect a fence around the dog, or you could visualize a pet polar bear coming to your defense, or, best of all, you could simply put yourself on a sunlit Caribbean beach with no dogs in sight.

And speaking of sunlit Caribbean beaches, that's a great way to practice meditation. Close your eyes and picture the most beautiful spot you can think of. Visualize the heat of the sun, feel the sand between your toes, hear the waves crashing against the shore. Make it as real as you can. Or create a cool pine forest overlooking crystal-clear lakes, reflecting snowcapped mountain peaks. Smell the scent of the pine and hear the call of the wild geese. Create your vision anywhere you want, actual or imagined, present, past, or future. But visualize it so strongly that your senses are filled with its presence and it comes alive to your inner eye. Then, when you have it just the way you want it mentally, invite your favorite people to come, and feel their pleasure at being there with you. As with any meditation, if other thoughts enter your head, don't get angry or try to force them out; just forget them and return to your own personal Shangri-La.

This ability to control the thoughts that cross your mind is a goal of meditation. Its value in the bardo, a world of nonphysical thought forms, should be obvious.

Peace and love

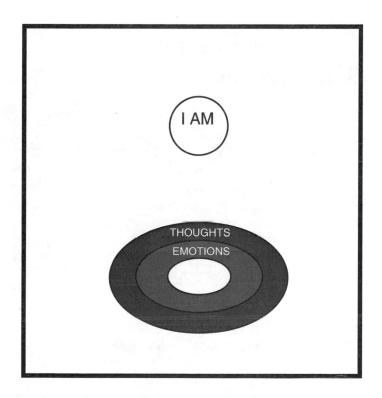

At some point in the bardo, all of your individual presence and personality layers fall away. You are still very much alive. You are at your absolute perfect core. You have no adjectives to limit or describe you, but you can still feel "I Am. . . ."

14
Background to the
Bardo Thödol

Dear friend,

We've covered quite a bit of ground in these letters so far, starting with the nature of death and an understanding of its limitation to the physical realm. We have developed a feeling for life beyond the body, based on the firsthand experiences and reports of people whose bodies have been medically resuscitated after death. We've even pointed towards your own inner doorway and taught a number of meditation techniques which should help you go inside and become more familiar with the eternal part of you which will survive when the body drops off. All this is by way of introduction.

Now it is time to present the actual material which will provide you with the guidelines and the road map for your upcoming journey. The source of the information you will be reading is twelve hundred years old, but it is as new as today, for like the Bible, it is an ageless thing that comes alive when it is put into practice. It is universal. It is applicable to all people at all times, yet it was developed by a race physically separate and isolated from the rest of the world. And though it was put into writing by a great holy man and teacher, in its present context it does not demand any specific religious dogma or particular point of view.

It is the *Bardo Thödol,* a Buddhist work, and one of the most mysterious and misunderstood books ever written. Since it is to play such an important part in what is to follow, I feel it is valuable that you know at least a little about its fascinating origin and the culture which brought it to life.

As Christianity grew out of Judaism because of the teachings of Jesus the Christ, so Buddhism grew out of Hinduism as a result of the teachings of Gautama the Buddha.

Siddartha Gautama was born into a royal family in an area now part of Nepal, in the sixth century B.C. Shielded by his father from anything which could possibly cause him unhappiness, he spent his early years in luxury, surrounded not only by servants but by a high wall built around the royal enclave further separating him from the reality of life. When, in his twenties, he first learned of the existence of illness, aging, and suffering, he was moved by an intense compassion and love to find the source of that unhappiness and to relieve it not only for himself but for all people.

The young Siddartha left his home and began many years of wandering as a sannyasin, a penniless Hindu monk, attempting to find the meaning of life, and from that, the source of human suffering. After starving and torturing his body in an attempt to achieve the understanding he desired, one day he realized that this extreme of penance was no different from the extreme of self-indulgence he had previously known. Moderating his views, he adopted a life style he called the Middle Way, neither torturing nor indulging his body but treating it merely as the vehicle in which he was experiencing his particular existence on this planet.

Unhappiness, Gautama realized, is part of the very essence of our existence. However, it is not the experiences we have in life that cause it. Rather, unhappiness is actually created by our cravings, desires, and expectations of what we want life to be. If we desire riches, poverty makes us unhappy. If we desire youth, old age makes us unhappy. If we cannot accept the inevitable change which marks the nature of existence, unhappiness cannot be avoided. However, selfish desire can be destroyed, and it is only the person who can do this and face all of life's realities with poise and equanimity who can truly enjoy existence and lead a fulfilling and happy life. Gautama developed a philosophy of peace from within based on an eightfold path of right understanding, right purpose, right speech, right conduct, right vocation, right effort, right alertness, and right concentration. He spent the last forty years of his life teaching what he had found, and eventually died in his eighties in the arms of one of his disciples.

With the death of the Buddha, a term which means "perfected one," his philosophy continued to spread throughout Asia, with changes and modifications as it grew. It finally entered Tibet in the seventh century A.D. as a result of royal marriages with princesses from Nepal and China.

In Tibet, Buddhism found itself superimposed on Bön, the native religion, a highly charged complex of demons and deities who were both dangerous and beneficent. Accordingly, the levels of understanding an individual needed to pass through to reach the highest truth were visualized as being populated by spirits. Each of these had its own particular purpose, and each interacted with the seeker, leading him towards or away from his avowed goal. Thus, in Tibet, the subtlety of the Buddhist teaching that all thoughts and visions come from within the mind of the individual was combined with the shamanistic idea of external spirits, a concept easier for the general population to grasp.

In the eighth century, Padma Sambhava, a professor of yoga at the Buddhist university of Nalanda, India, was invited by the Tibetan king to come to Tibet. Now when we call Padma Sambhava a "professor" of yoga, we should understand that this meant more than such a title would today. Indeed, Padma Sambhava was actually known as a great master of the occult, and as his first duty to his new benefactor he was required to exorcise demons from an area where the king wished to build a monastery. This was done and Padma Sambhava established the first community of Tibetan monks, or lamas, in 749 A.D. It was he who first put the *Bardo Thödol* into writing.

Peace and love

15
The Tibetan Book of the Dead

Dear friend,

In the last letter we looked at the historical setting within which Padma Sambhava, the founder of Tibetan Lamaism, created the *Bardo Thödol*, a book which has remained a cornerstone of the Tibetan culture for over a thousand years. Its teachings about the many pathways which the individual soul can take after death are a fascinating combination of the Buddha's concept of the totality of existence being within the individual consciousness and the various aspects of that consciousness, represented by the numerous gods, spirits, and settings known and accepted by the practitioners of Bön. In some ways it is this very dichotomy between the highly intellectual and the intensely ritualistic which provides the book's great emotional and inspirational impact, not to mention its unique and colorful cast of characters.

The first English translation was done some twelve hundred years after Padma Sambhava, by the joint effort of the Tibetan lama Kazi Dawa Samdup and the British scholar W. Y. Evans-Wentz. Born in 1868 at Kalimpong of native hillsmen, Kazi Dawa Samdup attended school in Darjeeling and entered the service of the British government as an interpreter at Baxe Duar in Bhutan. A highly spiritual man, Dawa Samdup was fluent in both the ways of the West and the mystical calling of his native country. At the time of the translation, he was the headmaster of the government's school for boys at Gangtok. However, it is reported that his wanderings into the spiritual world, following in the footsteps of his guru, the hermit Norbu, distracted him more than a little from his duties at the school. While this may have proved distressing to the government officials who paid his salary, it is of interest to note that it is in the area of this, his avocation, that his greatest contribution to humanity was made.

The relationship between the two men was symbiotic. On the one hand, Evans-Wentz was acknowledged by the Tibetan as his "living English dictionary," while the Englishman admitted in turn that his knowledge of Tibetan was "almost as nothing." Nevertheless, the two worked closely to keep the meaning and the sense of the idiomatic structure of the translation as close to the original as the Tibetan and English tongues would permit. In 1920, Dawa Samdup was appointed lecturer in Tibetan at the University of Calcutta, where he died two years later, unable to accustom himself to the tropical climate of the lowlands, and without seeing the final fruits of his labors.

Evans-Wentz, meanwhile, brought the completed text to England where it was published in 1927 by the Oxford University Press. Since then it has been used for virtually all the translations which have been made into other Western languages, and though more recent versions have been undertaken, this first one remains to this day, through numerous reprints, the definitive English text.

However, even Evans-Wentz recognized in his introduction to the first edition that "in years to come, it is quite possible that our rendering...may be subject to revision. A strictly literal rendering of a work so abstruse in its real meanings as this, and written in symbolical language as well, if attempted by Europeans...would, perhaps, be as misleading as some of their renderings of the ancient Sanskrit vedas." Evans-Wentz accepted that intellectual openness and honesty are required in working with the original text. However, communication through translation is more than merely an understanding of and feeling for what the source document has to say. An equally critical factor is the ability to relate those thoughts to the frame of reference of the receiving language and culture. Hence, an important translated work must be constantly updated, in the same way that the Bible is periodically revised; not so as to change its meaning, but just the reverse—to hold the meaning and ultimate message inviolate.

It was Evans-Wentz who gave the book its English title, *The Tibetan Book of the Dead,* and it is worthwhile to dwell on this name for just a moment, since the mood which a title sets can definitely affect one's attitude towards the work. I can remember when I was a boy back in the late 1940s lying in bed one night listening to a drama on the radio. Although the details are long gone, I can still recall the feeling which coursed through my body as the hero and heroine, lost from the rest of their party during a trek through the Himalayas, stumble upon a little hut where they are allowed to stay the night. While the hermit who lives there goes out to fetch some water, the travelers take the time to look around at their surroundings. Suddenly, there is a gasp. "What is it, Neville?" the heroine asks, her voice quaking in fear. Neville, who is on leave from the university and can read a number of Asiatic scripts, is breathing hard. "My God, Nora, the book he's reading. It's... *The Tibetan Book of the Dead!!!*" Music up and fade out to the commercial.

The word *bardo* as we have already noted means "intermediate state" or "place in between," both of which are fairly innocuous and definitely nonthreatening. *Thödol* can be translated as "book," and so we have a literal translation of *Bardo Thödol* into "book of the intermediate state." However, with such a title one needs to understand something of what the intermediate state is. Since nothing in Western thought even comes close to that term, such a title clearly falls short. Also, the literal translation is definitely not designed to sell books, and so perhaps it was one of Oxford's editors and not Evans-Wentz who came up with the final choice. In any case, whatever the name and whoever is responsible for it, it is important that you accept the book without fear or prejudice for its highly positive, highly spiritual teachings. To its devotees, it is a work designed to guide them both in the bardo and in their lives on Earth as well.

Peace and love

16
God as Self

Dear friend,

As we make final preparations prior to entering and exploring the bardo, there are several bits of information you should have which will help you understand more clearly exactly what is going on around you. The first of these involves the basic question of who is actually running the show, and what our personal relationship is to this Source of all power and creation.

In this area Western religious devotees have traditionally held a fundamental belief that is somewhat different from those of Easterners. While both recognize an ultimate Source of universal energy, followers of Judaism and Christianity tend to view that Source as something separate from and outside of themselves. They call it God and point to it up in the sky. Thus, the search for spiritual truth becomes more of a penance to be served in the hope that if they follow proper actions and rituals this all-powerful God will grant them the rewards of peace and plenty on Earth, and eternal happiness in heaven.

Hindus and Buddhists, on the other hand, accept the universal nature of this Source, but also view it as existing within every one of us. Hindus actually recognize these two aspects of God by the use of two different words: *Brahman* for the universal aspect and *Atman* for the individual aspect. The Buddha never spoke of God at all, focusing his teachings on the need for individuals to touch base with their own inner core. In either case the search for spiritual truth evolves into the challenge of recognizing total existence and presence within, and viewing everything that occurs in life as being part of that totality. Accordingly, the spiritual seeker attempts to remove his weaknesses and clean up his act, not so that he may receive the bounty of an external God, but so that he may experience the reality of the power which already exists within him.

It is true that throughout history many Westerners have felt God within them and have made this feeling known. Indeed, this is the message that Jesus shared when he said, "The Father lives in me." Unfortunately for others as well as for Jesus, for almost the next two thousand years such pronouncements often meant martyrdom from a hierarchy more interested in dogma than in wisdom. Today, however, we are at a point in history where such individual searches for truth are not likely to end up at the stake. In fact, an increasing number of aspirants in the West are turning inward to find that truth within which Jesus actually taught, and which for centuries Eastern devotees have known exists.

This, in fact, is one of the major hallmarks of the New Age, the recognition that the light in one is the light in all, and that the ultimate responsibility for our lives and our actions lies with us and our own choices, and does not depend upon the whim of an all-powerful outsider who can do with us as he wills. Not only does this allow us truly to design and create our lives as we see fit, but when we all assume full responsibility for our actions, we will also find that what has been created is that ever-elusive Peace on Earth.

This difference in perspective is seen most clearly in the concept of improper action, what is commonly referred to as "sin." To the Westerner, sin is doing something "wrong," that is, acting in a way that is not approved by God. The problem with this view is that one person's opinion of right and wrong may not be the same as someone else's, and it becomes difficult, if not impossible, to determine whose "right" is really what God had in mind. The result is that right becomes a function of whoever is in power at the time.

To the Easterner, the only "sin," if we can use that word at all, is ignorance, that is, lack of knowledge about God manifesting on Earth through you. This line of reasoning says that if you know God exists within, you cannot help but lead a good and proper life.

Sri Ramakrishna, the nineteenth century yogi, illustrates this point with a beautiful little story of the robber who was ransacking a temple when his noises aroused the attention of a holy man who entered the temple and caught him in the act.

"What are you doing?" asked the holy man.

"I am robbing the temple," answered the robber, "but, alas, I am not a good robber since my actions aroused your attention."

"Ah," replied the holy man, "God is the only source of perfection there is. If you will but keep God constantly in your mind, you will achieve perfection and become the perfect robber."

"Thank you for the advice," answered the robber. "I will do as you say," and loading his booty into a sack, he left.

One week later he returned to the temple and knelt at the feet of the holy man.

"You tricked me," he said, "for when I placed God's vision before my eyes I was no longer able to be a robber." And returning all of the stolen goods to the temple, he became the holy man's disciple, living in God's vision for the rest of his life.

The moral is simple. Stealing is not a part of the nature of perfection. Hold that perfection in your mind, therefore, and you cannot steal, for imperfect thoughts and actions cannot exist in a perfect setting. On the other hand, if you continue to be a robber, you must not be focusing on perfection. So it is in life and so it will be in the bardo.

Peace and love

17
The Tibetan cosmology

Dear friend,

Unlike the adherents of traditional Judeo-Christian teachings, Tibetans consider the ultimate destination of their soul to be an absolute merging with the Godhead, the fount of all creation. Yes, it has truly been there all along, but the trick is to know it, live it, and make it your reality rather than continue to visualize yourself in your individual form with your individual limitations. Even the concept of being in heaven "at the feet of God" means that you still feel a separation between yourself and God. From that perspective, heaven becomes only a stopping place on the path, not yet a final destination. In such a case, something is blocking your acceptance of the absolute perfection which does exist within you since God is, you are, and you are one. Eventually, therefore, you must return to life in a new body to "take up where you left off" and get rid of the elements of imperfection within you. And since time is not a question where God is concerned, this process could go on and on and on.

Even more remarkable to the Westerner unfamiliar with Eastern thinking is the fact that your next destination after death is not a reward/punishment decision made by an external God sitting in judgment of you. Rather, it is determined by a function of your own personality as indicated by the mental state you are in at the moment of death. If you are meditating on God, that is, on your highest self, you will reach the highest goal, the merging of your Self with Universal Consciousness. This is called nirvana, though of course, it is immaterial what you name it. If you feel fear, anger, jealousy, hatred, and so forth, you will be led through the bardo towards the area of the afterlife catering to those particular emotions. The *Bardo Thödol* speaks of six different realms into which your spirit may emerge upon passing through the bardo. Each has its own particular set of characteristics and requirements for entry; and each will be discussed separately in future letters.

As previously mentioned, the *Bardo Thödol* is a composite of the universal teachings of the Buddha overlaid on the shamanistic beliefs of the native Tibetan Bön. And so while the original requires the reader to become familiar with the names, attributes, and personalities of the whole cast of characters, it is certainly not necessary for the contemporary Western seeker to learn them in order to benefit from the book's universal teachings. In fact, there is even question among modern-day Tibetan lamas as to what images the Westerner will experience in the deeper recesses of the bardo.

For while these different realms are given names, attributes, locations, and reigning deities and are treated as actual physical places, consciousness is the only true absolute reality. Thus, the six realms are no more nor less than states of mind experienced by individual souls whose natural bent, as demonstrated during life on Earth, will lead them to one or another of these psychological states. And since basic human pulls, drives, and instincts are the same through all time, though the trappings vary in different cultures, the maze of pathways you traverse from the moment of death until the emergence of your individual soul on the other side of the bardo is laid out here as it appears in the Tibetan original. But symbolism is used only as a signpost and as an aid in portraying the feeling and power which the original was designed to invoke. Accordingly, if you honestly take a look at yourself as we wander through the bardo together, you should be able to get an advance picture of where your particular personality will lead you when practice becomes reality.

It is legitimate to wonder why the Tibetans have recognized and accepted this highly sophisticated framework of the eternal inner life of the soul for well over a thousand years while we in the West are still stumbling at the doorstep of spiritual understanding. The answer is really quite logical.

Any given people develop to a great extent as a result of the surroundings and situations in which it finds itself. Climatic and geophysical conditions make one land suitable for farming while another is ideal for cattle grazing or for gathering abundance from the sea. There are areas of the Earth where food products grow wild without the need for cultivation, and in those regions the populace is less motivated to work than in those places where food is scarce. It follows, then, that where life is easy, people are less inclined to make the effort to figure out what it is all about. Practically speaking, we tend to question the meaning of life more when we are cold and hungry and tired than when we are lying on a sun-drenched beach sipping a piña colada.

In Tibet there are no sun-drenched beaches. Flat grassy tablelands, jagged peaks, howling winds, and snows which isolate villages for six months or more out of the year are standard fare. Just keeping alive and well-fed takes monumental effort. Distances between pockets of civilization are great, and individuals must find that resource within to ensure their survival through long

70

periods of cold and isolation. But that same isolation coupled with the majestic beauty of the Himalayan peaks has served to turn Tibetans inward, so they seek comfort and ultimate purpose not in external belongings and the ease of physical life, but in peace of mind and knowledge of how they fit into the whole universal scheme of things.

While Westerners have tended to concentrate on understanding and taming the physical world, Tibetans have gone inside to understand and tame the spiritual world. It is as natural that they should discover the reality of spiritual life as that we should put a man on the moon. It's just a question of where you place your priorities.

Peace and love

18
Meditation techniques

Dear friend,

Practice being at peace. The value of your being relaxed, of having both your mind and body at ease, is that it allows you to cast away every fear, anxiety, and concern about what is going to happen. I have mentioned this numerous times already in these letters, but there is no way I can overemphasize its importance once you die and enter the bardo. Practice meditation whenever you can so that you get proficient in overcoming fear and replacing it with peace. And note that replacing fear with peace is different from fighting the fear or trying to overcome it by sheer willpower. When you do the latter you remain tense, for you are still acknowledging fear's presence. Simply become peaceful and fear will no longer be a part of you. It is a major step in learning to control what lies ahead.

Stop for a moment and see how you feel right now. Are you tense or are you relaxed? Are you defensive and fearful, or are you open and positive? Please examine not only your physical feelings, but your mental ones and your emotions, for these are the parts that will accompany you on your upcoming journey.

You have been working on getting inside of your head and closing the doors to the outside. You have also learned how to still the many noises in your own mind by focusing on only one thought, thereby removing your concentration from all the other thoughts which are clamoring for your attention. I don't know what primitive people experienced in this area, whether it was pictures or lights or images, or whatnot. But for us, twentieth-century Western intellectuals, it's words, words, words, and it hurts just thinking about it.

Even if you sit quietly, cut off from the madhouse disco raging all around you, you're still sure to hear full phrases and sentences spilling over unbidden into your consciousness. "What's for dinner?" "I wonder how long I've been sitting here," "Hey, I haven't had a thought for over a minute!" All these and more just come spewing out as if your mind were the vacuum that nature abhors.

* Don't fight these thoughts. This is very important. If you do, then you are just substituting one thought for another. "What's for dinner?" becomes transformed into, "I'm not going to think about food, I'm not going to think about food, I'm not..."etc., etc. But the ultimate goal is not to modify the subject of your inner conversations, but to eliminate them altogether. Also, fighting within yourself just creates more tension and, as you recall, relaxation is the reason you are doing this in the first place.

There are literally hundreds of different methods which are touted as being able to rid the mind of these uninvited intruders. For me they all boil down to two basic techniques, and we've already discussed one of them, focusing. The other one is *emptying*, and that's what this letter is about. Try them both; modify them to your needs and see what feels right for you.

Emptying is cleaning out the inkwell without pouring water in or dumping the ink out, without using any cleaning techniques at all. You simply say, "The inkwell is empty," and take it from there. This is more like the Zen way of doing it. At first, however, some visualization may be necessary, and you might try the following technique to get an idea of what emptying feels like.

Close your eyes and see yourself sitting on the bottom of a swimming pool. Your mind is blank, you have no thoughts, you have no mind, you just are. Don't think of anything, don't think of nothing, just don't think. There *is* a difference. When you find a thought developing, simply put it into an air bubble and let it rise out the top of your head to the surface, far above your mental image. Note that the key is that you have not forced the idea out, you have simply let it float away on its own. Go back to not thinking. Do this as often as is necessary. Soon the bubbles will be rising to the surface of the water before you even have the chance to see the thought inside of them. Become carbonated. You will emerge from these underwater excursions totally rested and at ease. Then, once you have felt what it is like to have your thoughts go away without effort, you'll be able to retain that empty state without the image of the swimming pool.

By now your own experiences should have demonstrated that meditation is completely nonsectarian and has nothing at all to do with one religion or another. Hindus, Buddhists, Christians, Jews, Muslims, agnostics, atheists, or anyone else can meditate without its conflicting in any way with what they have been taught or what they might believe. All you are trying to do is to close off the pressures of the outer world long enough to find the door to the inner one. And that inner door does exist within each one of us, no matter what our religious beliefs or philosophic inclinations.

Looking at it from that perspective you should now be able to relate to those scenes in travelogues of mountaintop monasteries with row upon row of orange-robed monks with shaved heads, squatting silently facing blank white walls, their eyes closed, saying nothing, with visions of ecstasy written upon their faces. There isn't much external pressure on top of a mountain, and so it's a perfect place to practice meditation. These seekers, deep in meditation, are not propounding any specific religion or dogma. In fact, they are probably not even focusing on the same thing, if they are focusing on anything at all. They are merely practicing and experiencing emptying, shutting off the external senses while tuning in to their individual inner worlds. They are getting in touch with the part of them which will outlive their bodies, the part of you which will outlive your death.

Peace and love

The "I Am. . ." which you experience at your absolute perfect core is the same "I Am. . ." which is experienced by all people at their core. It is Universal Consciousness. It is God. You can only truly feel it when you do not limit yourself by personality layers.

19
The moment of death

Dear friend,

Feel the scene. You are lying in your bed. There may or may not be people around you. It doesn't matter, for your thoughts are inside yourself waiting for the inner signs you know will come and signal the steps which are to follow. You are relaxed, you are at peace, you know that what is about to happen is right and natural. You have read these words, and you remember the sequence of events you will be experiencing. You have no fear. You know that when it is all over you will still be very much alive.

The actual process of separation from your body takes place in a number of steps, much the same way that clothing is removed prior to going to sleep. And just as heavier outer clothing is taken off before the more delicate inner clothing, so it is with the various elements which connect us through the body to the physical world. Our awareness separates from the outside in and occurs in the same sequence for all people. How long any one part of the process will last or how clearly you will be able to recognize it as it is happening is impossible to say. That depends on the nature and speed of different causes of death, and the use of drugs and painkillers which can affect consciousness and inner awareness.

The first element to be removed is the grossest and most solid, earth. You should feel a growing weakness in body and limbs and a bodily sensation of pressure described by the *Bardo Thödol* as "earth sinking into water." Sight will dim, and you may see mirages and have the impression of falling or of sensing earthquakes.

This is followed by the loss of the water element, manifested as a bodily sensation of clammy coldness merging into feverish heat, "water sinking into fire." You will feel thirst. Hearing will also become unclear as your consciousness continues to become detached from your surroundings. Your inner vision may appear smoky, and you may feel as if flooding has encompassed the world.

Next is "fire sinking into air," a feeling as if the body were being separated into atoms. Breathing will become more difficult. You will lose your body heat and sense of smell. You may feel that the entire world is on fire, and you may see tiny sparks of light in your inner vision.

Finally the air itself dissolves into ether, or energy, and your last ties to Earth are about to be severed. The feelings you have are very subtle as you undergo the loss of taste, the sensation of touch, and the cessation of any thought of the external world. You may begin to hear an internal thunder-like roar and experience the dimming of your individual internal lights as all begins to dissolve into oneness.

Documented contemporary death experiences indicate that these transitional states occur without pain, thus facilitating the focusing of your consciousness on where you are headed rather than on where you are coming from. This is important, for during this transitional period you should consciously focus on the life to which you are going, rather than trying to cling tenaciously to the physical life you are leaving behind.

In Tibet, where the role of the clergy is to aid and

guide the dying individual from one side to the other, the attending lamas will sit by the bed, softly repeating over and over the conditions which the person should be experiencing as the dying process progresses. Lamas will even gently yet firmly press the arteries on either side of the neck, if necessary, so that the individual does not fall asleep, but remains fully aware and conscious of everything that is happening to him. With pain gone, full awareness, prior knowledge of what to expect, and an attending guide at the bedside, the dying person is in the best position to make a successful passage and get to the place in the bardo where he wants to be.

Even after he is sure the soul and the body have separated, the lama will remain by the bedside, constantly reminding the disembodied soul of what it should be encountering and what its next actions should be. Given the knowledge we now have about the ability of the newly deceased spirit to hear what is being said in the vicinity of its former body, the practice seems to make sense.

We in the West, unfortunately, do not have this same type of relationship with our spiritual advisors. Indeed, they spend their energy in trying to comfort the living, while leaving the newly deceased soul to fend for itself. Thus, we face a death where pain has been deadened by drugs which kill awareness, no one knows what to expect, and the only attendants at the bedside are fighting to keep the inevitable from occurring. However, I predict that this will change shortly as the reality of the bardo and the true spiritual needs of the deceased individual become more widely understood and accepted in the West. Until then each one of us is on our own, as we will be, in the final analysis, throughout the bardo.

The "advice" that the lama gives takes the form of a prayer which the newly deceased soul is reminded to focus on and repeat, with the knowledge that in the bardo thought is the reality and prayer the means of locomotion. It translates roughly as follows:

> Oh, this is now the hour of death. I resolve to direct all my effort towards love and compassion so as to obtain perfect Godhood. For by so doing, I will be acting for the good of all sentient beings throughout the universe.

What a beautiful thought.

Peace and love

20
The clear light dawns

Dear friend,

Just prior to the cessation of your breathing, in your mind's eye you will see a clear light like a void and cloudless sky. During a peaceful, gradual dying process this clear light can even dawn for as long as twenty minutes to half an hour before the actual cessation of breath. It will be perfect, spotless, and pure, and will appear as a transparent vacuum without center or circumference. It will fill every single part of your being with its presence and will be the brightest, clearest light you have ever seen. It is the first major landmark you will encounter in the bardo, the point at which the Tibetans calculate that quantitative change has become qualitative, and death can be considered to have occurred.

This dawning of the clear light, as you have already read, has been documented by people brought back from clinical death by modern science. It is normally described as appearing at the end of a long tunnel through which the soul seems to be traveling. This is due to the fact that the light first becomes visible to your inner eye as a tiny pinpoint, which keeps growing and growing until it fills your entire being. It is what you would perceive visually if you were in a tunnel focusing your attention on the tiny light at the far end. To your eye, it would get larger and larger until you finally traveled through to the end and emerged into bright clear sunlight.

But the light is more than just light. It is the light as in "Let there be light," the Ultimate Reality, the big bang, the pleroma, the Source of all. Those who have experienced it during both death return experiences and advanced meditation techniques describe their sensing it as a being, a consciousness, or a presence which fills them not with fear or foreboding, but with intense peace and love. They feel immeasurable power, something so strong, so peaceful, so undefinable and all-encompassing that it cannot be limited by giving it a name. The characteristic consciousness felt at this moment of transition is that of a void, not the void of nothingness, but more like the bare intellect: unobstructed, shining, thrilling, and blissful, the very consciousness of God. This is the power which changes our lives simply by knowing of its existence.

But this God, this Power, is not something that exists apart from you although it's only natural to think so the first time you face it. What has actually happened at that moment when you encounter the light is that you have been stripped of all your impurities, all of your limiting individual personality characteristics; you have been shown the true nature of your being and have been offered the immediate opportunity to exist for all time in your ultimate perfection. Another way of looking at it, particularly if you still view God as being outside of yourself, is that the Ultimate Source of all reality and the energy behind universal creation has come to you, revealed itself to you, and offered you the opportunity to merge with it for the rest of eternity.

This feeling of oneness with God is what all sentient beings subconsciously seek. But in the same way that a baby born into the physical world must wake up to its new surroundings, you, the newly deceased soul, must wake up to where you now find yourself. If you can recognize your condition and remain there, the journey is over. Eternal perfection and peace, heaven, the kingdom of God, nirvana, the happy hunting ground—call it what you will—it has been achieved. You are home.

However, as you have been forewarned, the ability to control your thoughts at this important moment and to hold your consciousness firmly on the light of creation is a function of the knowledge and experience which you have gained and practiced during your Earthly life. If you are a devout person, or an experienced meditator, or even one who has merely read and become familiar with the basic factual material presented on these pages, you will have a much easier time of recognizing the clear light for what it is. As a result of having come into contact with the light while still alive, you will have a much smoother transition into the dying state than one who has not contemplated the eternal during his lifetime and therefore fears and tries to avoid this dawning of the unknown.

It is important to reemphasize here that the goal of ultimate eternal rest for the individual is the same for all souls, regardless of the type or level of faith they may have displayed during their lifetimes. However, if you have not had faith, have not expected to find life after death, and do not recognize the symptoms of death and dying, you will have a much more difficult time retaining the clear light of consciousness in your mind during this period of transition. As a result, your thoughts will stray away from the light to other images, and you will slip from this place of perfection to other locations in the bardo.

Once death has actually occurred, consciousness of the clear light can remain for as long as three-and-a-half to four days, although for those who have led an

evil life or are of unsound nerves it may be only as long
as it would take to "snap a finger." But to remain in
that place, your mind must not stray. You must know
and feel that this condition is your true character, your
true Self, and that your individuality and personality
must be sublimated into total oneness with all creation.
Consciousness is not lost, only individuality. It is what
the yogi means when he says, "You are a drop of water.
God is the ocean. Fall into the ocean. The drop disap-
pears. Become the ocean."

Peace and love

21
The secondary light

Dear friend,

The fear of losing their individuality and the subconscious desire to maintain their unique personality are the reasons why the majority of souls are unable to hold onto the primary clear light and remain in the heavenly state. Even highly devout persons who have lived a good and holy life can face this consequence of their own thoughts. By continuing to think as the specific individual they were while alive, and being unable to focus on God without form, they voluntarily separate themselves from total God-consciousness without really knowing what they are doing and what they are losing. They pass to the point in the bardo where the secondary light dawns.

Similarly, on the other end of the scale, the untrained, unaware individual may find herself in a somewhat different situation which leads to the same result. With her consciousness now existing outside and independent of her physical body, she will begin to wonder what is happening. "Am I dead or am I not dead?" She will see relatives, be aware of their crying and carrying on, and will be confused, especially if she hadn't realized that life would continue after her body died. To her, the clear light and what it represents may be just a blinding annoyance, and she may actually go out of her way to escape from the glare. She, too, will slip to the next level, impelled downward by her own lack of knowledge.

It is interesting to note that the Tibetans believe most strongly that any bedside demonstrations of sadness or grief will tend to draw the consciousness of the deceased back to its former physical existence, rather than leaving it free and unburdened to travel in the new realm in which it finds itself. Thus, the weeping and wailing found at most Western deathbeds is expressly forbidden. It also explains the story of the dying old woman who called her grown children to her side, thanked them for being a part of her life, blessed them, and then told them to get out and stay out. "I've devoted my life to your futures," she said. "Now I want to concentrate strictly on mine."

If the deceased had realized during her lifetime that Oneness with God means loss of individuality, she would have been at what the Tibetans call the "perfected" stage. In that instance, the lama would continue his previous instructions to meditate on the clear light. If, however, the deceased had been at the "visualizing" stage, had realized and accepted God as something outside of and separate from her own being, more like the typical Westerner, then on an average of half-an-hour after the cessation of breath, a secondary clear light would dawn. Such a soul is instructed by the lamas to meditate on her "tutelary deity," the vision which accompanies that light. Heaven is still attainable in its ultimate eternal form, but the individual is now at the stage where she needs help to retain it.

According to the dictionary, the word "tutelary" is defined as "having the position of guardian or protector of a person, place, or thing." The dictionary even gives the phrase "tutelary saint" as being an example of proper usage. Thus, under that definition, Saint Patrick is Ireland's "tutelary deity." However it is interesting to note that the Tibetan word which has been translated into English as "tutelary deity" is "yidam," and that actually means something a bit different, something rather unique to Western thinking.

To the Tibetan, a yidam is not just an external protector but actually the entity or being which is the individual's personal representation of her own concept of perfection. In its most simplistic form, therefore, a person's yidam could be viewed as the one that person would choose to be if she could be anyone, human or deity, in the whole universe. Now this should be looked at as more than just wishful thinking or a childish game. Try to follow the logic in the next several paragraphs, and you will soon see how this concept has a dramatic and most important message for you and every other person hearing of this for the first time.

As we have discussed earlier, the Eastern devotee is aware of the fact that the spark of life which animates her body is the same spark of life which animates all bodies. In other words, God exists within each individual and manifests differently through each one's existence. But the devotee is also aware that she has been subject during her life to the pulls and temptations of other than her purest, most godly interests. She knows that, although she may be a good person most of the time and able to focus on God's light some of the time, there are numerous instances each day when she catches herself in an ungodly thought or action.

So she has chosen a yidam, a godly entity to represent her image of perfection. This is her idea of the manifest God, the one she will pray to and whose image will appear in her mind's eye during meditation. This is the being she will focus on in time of need or stress, for this is the one who represents her in her most perfect state, free from worldly impurities. This is the being who behaves at all times the way she would always like to behave. Therefore, this is the being she will attempt to merge with in the bardo.

The logic here is obvious. Since you know that your yidam is always in a state of God-consciousness, if you can only merge and become one with its mental image, you will experience the perfection that it is experiencing, and remain in eternal God-consciousness yourself. This is meditation on God with form, and it transports the individual to the same high state of eternal Universal Consciousness as meditation on the light, or God without form, does. However, once again, the ability to remain in that state is a function of the experience you have gained while alive.

Peace and love

22
Jesus the Christ

Dear friend,

In Tibet, as throughout the entire East, the yidam can be chosen from a wide panoply of deities, each representing a specific aspect of personality. None is right, none is wrong, and you are free to select whichever is in particular harmony with your inner feelings, whichever feels right for you. Nor should you assume that you have peaked at a less than holy state if you feel the need for a concrete aid in the visualization of perfection. It is not easy to meditate on something as nebulous and undefinable as light. That is the case for most people, and this is where the value of the yidam, the individual idea of personal perfection, comes into play, for it permits us to visualize a three-dimensional God.

Westerners can have a choice of forms for God as well, for we are free to direct our prayers and concentrate our meditations on any number of saints, patriarchs, angels, or other holy beings. No matter whom we choose, if that being is truly focused on God and you can focus on him or her, you cannot help but get to the place where he or she is going.

One tutelary deity, however, has become the most popular by far. He is Jesus the Christ, and it is here at the visualizing stage of the secondary light that his teachings are fulfilled for the faithful. If you accept Jesus as your representation of perfection, your savior, yidam, or tutelary deity, call it what you will, you will surely find him when the primary clear light fades and the secondary light dawns. And, of course, he will lead you to the heaven of eternal rest and eternal peace.

The mechanics of how this actually works are truly interesting and something The Bible doesn't go into. However, the *Bardo Thödol* does explain it all, and it is a beautiful and perfect example of how universal truth transcends individual differences between people when the teachings of one master explain and agree with the teachings of another master, even though they are separated by thousands of miles and almost a thousand years.

It's really quite simple, as all truth is. Two thousand years ago there was a man known as Jesus of Nazareth who was born on Earth with the ability to focus his internal attention on the unceasing inner light of God. He could feel his eternal tie to his fellowman, his tie to all creation, and also his tie to the Source of all power, that which created what he saw and felt around him. He could always do this, no matter what was happening to him in the physical world. No one in the entire history of the Jews, the people into whom he was born, had ever demonstrated such abilities before.

So strong was the pull of the light of God within this man that other people could feel its presence through him. They flocked to be near him, to touch him, to have him teach them about the power that radiated from him like a living being. Although he was treated cruelly and unjustly by men of lesser understanding, he never lost his faith in the God within. He became a symbol of all that is good, all that is godly, all that is perfect on Earth. He became known as Jesus the Christ, *Christos* being the Greek word meaning "light."

Jesus showed it was possible for us to know the inner

light of God while we are still very much a part of the physical world around us. Jesus was illumined. Not only at his death but throughout his entire life the primary light of God remained firmly fixed in his consciousness. That is why everything he did flowed and was right and represented the ultimate good. That is what made him different. He absolutely and completely sublimated the ego of Jesus the carpenter and rabbi to his role as Jesus the Christ, the God Being connected to total Universal Consciousness. He lived as that inner God led him, not as he, as an individual ego, might necessarily have wished.

As we have noted, it is easier to focus one's inner eye on something concrete rather than on something nebulous. Jesus did the hard part and the Christ Light now offers that opportunity to those who cannot hold onto the primary clear light. Simply focus on the vision of this beautiful soul who not only knew where the light came from but where it was going, and you will reach the same destination he reached. You will merge with him, just as he promised you would.

Other people in other times and cultures may use different illumined individuals to reach the same goal. They can fix their attention on Krishna the Light, or Buddha the Light, and become part of the ultimate oneness in the same way that someone who holds on to the image of Jesus the Light can. But the issue here is not whether any one yidam is better than any other. The real question is whether you have the strength of will to follow your chosen deity wherever you are led.

You could compare it to being part of a mountain-climbing expedition through treacherous terrain when a sudden blinding snowstorm strikes. Since you don't know the way, you rope yourself to your guide, and wherever he goes you follow. No matter where he leads you, whether it is across thin ledges or over deep crevasses, no matter how dangerous your situation appears, you must not separate yourself from him, nor can you give in to fear or lose your faith in his ability. If you do, you are lost.

So will it be following the Christ through the bardo, except that the rope holding you to him will be woven by the strength of your will and your prior practice. Do not be distracted. Earnestly focus and concentrate your mind on your yidam, as the reflection of the moon in the water, apparent yet inexistent in itself. Meditate upon Christ as if he were a being with a physical body, and if you hold firmly to your chosen vision, both your purpose and his promise will be fulfilled.

Peace and love

23
Meditation techniques

Dear friend,

I have meditated and studied for eleven years now in an attempt to learn about and understand the relationship between life and death. I am lucky. My odyssey started with enough desire to undertake the journey, yet enough daylight left for me to finish the trip while still alive. Not everyone has that luxury. Hopefully, however, this work may make it possible for you to reach that same plateau easier and faster, for someday you will find that what the Tibetan masters have taught is the truth. The greater your knowledge before you face that truth, the better.

Now breathe deeply, relax, and get into that calm space you have learned to reach through meditation. By now you should have found a technique that is comfortable for you. It doesn't matter what it is, and it doesn't matter whether or not anyone else in the world thinks that's the way it should be done. As long as it works for you, as long as it relaxes you and puts you at ease, it's right for you. Use it now. Get into a meditative state and take a moment to feel the sense of peace that pervades your whole body, your whole being.

Now I want you to visualize a light shining brilliantly inside your brain, the brightest, clearest light you have ever seen. It starts as a little pinpoint right at the very top of your head, and grows and grows until it fills every corner of your mind, every inch of your entire being. It is so bright you feel you are looking directly into the sun, yet there is no danger to your eyes because it is all happening inside your head. Look at the light with your inner eye and do not turn away. Feel that you are floating in space and the light is everywhere. Feel that the light is everything. Note how bright it is, how clear it is, how real it is. There is no center to the light, for it appears to radiate from everywhere at once. Hold on to that image as long as you can. Lose yourself in the light. Become the light. If you find yourself thinking about anything else at all, just stop and relax. Now go back and do it again.

That light you are trying to place and hold in your mind is the light of Universal Consciousness. That is the light reported by those who have had death return experiences. That is the light that met them, enfolded them, filled their spirits with peace and love, and gave them a new, deeper meaning and understanding of life. That is the light at the end of the tunnel, the one that met me ten years ago and changed forever the direction and purpose of my life. That is the light of God which touches everything it shines on and alters everything it touches.

That is the light which radiates from saints as an aura of peace and purity, and is depicted in art as a halo around their heads. That is the light of creation. That is the light which is the source of all power in the universe, the light of perfection and the absolute essence of mind. That is the light which exists within each of us. That is the light which defies description, and that is the light you will experience at the moment of death when your consciousness separates from your body.

It is not easy to meditate on something as nebulous and undefinable as light. Do not feel badly if you find

94

it slipping away, if you find other more concrete images and thoughts coming in to take its place. It happens that way to most people. However, I recently heard the story of a young boy who became totally blind at the age of eight. He was a sensitive youth, and as he lay in the hospital bed with bandages still covering his damaged eyes, his parents huddled together to figure out how to keep this highly developed intellect from drowning itself in self-pity. Entering his room, they approached their son with excitement, not sadness, in their voices. "You must be sure to tell us everything you experience in your new situation," they said. "Teach us what you learn."

Undistracted by external sights and fueled by his parents' encouragement, he began paying attention to the lights and images which appeared on the screen within his head, the images which do not require physical eyes to be seen. As the years went by, his diaries described the lights and colors he saw inside; how the light got brighter as his mood improved; how it disappeared completely during periods of anger. At age eleven, he wrote how sad he was for "sighted" boys and girls, who only view the dull external colors, not the bright internal ones. So proficient did he become in tuning in to the internal light that as an adult he found himself able to live among the seeing without assistance, guided only by the lights and images he saw projected on the dark blank screen of his mind, lights which were the auras of the objects in the physical world around him.

As we will discuss in subsequent letters, this ability to recognize and be guided by lights of various colors will play a vital role in your passage through the bardo. Unencumbered by physical eyes and external sights, you will be in the same position as the young man discussed above. But, unlike him, if you do not become familiar and comfortable with guidance by the internal light, you will not be able to move around the next realm or be in control of what happens there.

Therefore, it is extremely important that you learn to feel the presence of the clear white light while you are still alive. It is the foundation and source of everything else which will appear to you in the bardo, and the ultimate resting place of all living, sentient beings. Become comfortable with the light so that when it shines within and around you at the moment of death, you will welcome it and merge with it rather than fear it and try to escape its brilliance. Practice meditating on the light.

Peace and love

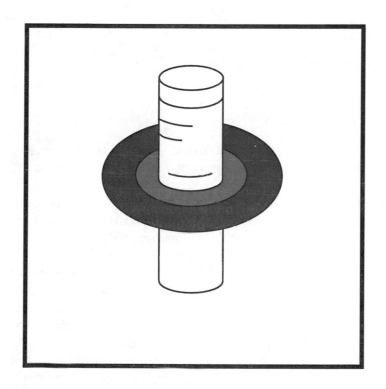

If you can accept and remain at one with Universal Conscious-ness, your trip is over. You will experience God for all eternity. Most people can't handle that. Individual thoughts, desires, and karmic debts break in to disturb the absolute peace. Old personal-ity layers re form in new ways. A new individual personality is arising.

24
The return of individuality

Dear friend,

At first the idea that all souls, good and evil, holy and unholy, get to experience even for a moment the bliss of perfection and the joy of heaven upon the body's death seems to be at odds with the teachings of mainstream Western religions. But think about it for a moment and you'll see that there's no disagreement here, only a slightly different way of looking at the same thing.

Heaven, you see, is not a short-term affair. Both Eastern and Western theology see it as eternal and timeless. Thus, an "unworthy" soul who encounters it briefly and then is carried off into other realms, through an inability to remain in the vision of the clear or secondary light, does not escape from a justly earned and deserved "punishment." Rather, like the child peering in the window of the candy store, the soul has been given a glimpse of something it will not be able to hold on to. That could prove to be a hell in and of itself, regardless of what the soul's future may be. However, you must always remember that the entire concept of life and existence is based not on fear and punishment, but on love and compassion, and a soul will be given numerous other opportunities to return to union and oneness with God if it cannot handle that at present.

Meanwhile, the reason a soul cannot merge with the

vision of light and perfection is that even though its core is perfection, part of its individual personality is not identical with that perfect nature. In other words, it has an aspect which is not love and compassion and which therefore makes it impossible for that soul to remain in an eternal state of oneness with a consciousness that is totally loving and compassionate.

The encounter with the light allows us, at least temporarily, to view our drives and desires from the third person, and to rise above them if we find them not to our liking. However, if the drives prove stronger than the desire for perfection, we end up in the position of the scorpion who asked the turtle to ferry him across the river.

"No way," said the turtle. "When I get to the middle of the river you'll sting me and I'll drown."

"Take off," answered the scorpion. "I'll be on your back. If you drown, I drown."

The turtle thought about it for a while and it sounded logical, so he agreed. The scorpion climbed on his back and off they swam across the river. Well, you guessed it. Right in the middle of the river the scorpion stung the turtle, who immediately reacted to the poison and began to sink with the scorpion still clinging to his back.

"Why'd you do it?" the turtle asked. "Now we'll both drown."

The scorpion shrugged. "Sorry," he responded, "that's just my nature."

Well, without taking the time and effort to step outside and see ourselves as we really are, we are simply acting like scorpions, following a "nature" which may or may not have our own best interests at heart. And, much like the scorpion who follows his nature with no regret or remorse for his actions, most of us behave the same way with regard to our drives, desires, fears, and motivations, both during our lifetimes and in the bardo.

Thus, after viewing and experiencing the light, most of us will find our individual personality characteristics starting to re-form around us. These are the drives and desires which motivated us during our lifetimes and which, while they may not be negative, nevertheless constitute the characteristics and attributes which make us unique, different, special, and one of a kind. If we carry them over into the bardo and do not wish to give them up, they will return to us, one by one. Gradually they will create layers of desire and individuality around us, and will lead us away from perfection towards another lifetime, where we will once again get the opportunity to recognize that we are as we are because we choose to be that way, not because we have to be that way.

Your own mind-set generated by the continuation of your Earthly personality will tend to draw you back to who you were. Like the dieter who dreams of jelly donuts, you will hear that little voice within urging you to return to ways you know you should leave behind. You will tend to follow that voice since it is your "nature," and as a result you will be led into whatever neighborhood caters to those wants and desires.

How could this occur when you know better than that, when you have already experienced the light of Universal Consciousness? Well, it's not as if you did something evil, consciously turning your back on the perfection of heaven. Chances are it's just that some other image, some other vision came into your mind, such as, "Where am I?"; "Am I really dead?"; "What will the family do without me?"; "There goes the business with Louie in charge!" Not bad thoughts, not evil thoughts, but not the thoughts which would cross the mind of either the formless God or your image of perfection, your yidam. Therefore, they pull you away from the light.

Now you can begin to see how this all relates to the idea of the devil, that evil force who gets the blame for humanity's weaknesses. Yes, our weaknesses are those factors that pull us away from the light. But those weaknesses are within us in just the same way that perfection is within us. There is no outside force to point to; our free will decides which way we go.

Peace and love

25
The fork in the road

Dear friend,

You have all the aspects of perfection within you. The life force which breathed in Moses, Jesus, Krishna, Buddha, and Muhammad breathes in you. In your absolute sense, at the very core of your being, you are perfection, just the way they were. You are God!

Until now most people never even suspected that God-Consciousness lives in them and experiences life in them through the feeling of "I Am" at their very core. In fact, God-Consciousness experiences life through every living being on the planet; each and every one of us. Masters have come to teach us that fact, but most people think too little of themselves to believe it could really be possible. Logically speaking, since it is only the God part of you that does exist in heaven, if you aren't familiar with what that God part of you feels like, how could you possibly remain in heaven even when the opportunity becomes available?

People tend to focus on their weaknesses and frailties rather than concentrate on their power and perfection. As a result they continue to make error after error, and then say, "What do you expect of me? I'm only a poor sinful human, I can't do any better." Even worse, as we mentioned at the very end of the previous letter, they blame all their calamities on some evil force outside of themselves: "The devil made me do it!" Nonsense. You made yourself do it! You have all the forces of the universe within you and are the one with the ultimate responsibility for how you run your life. That is the fork in the road you face every time you interact with the world around you. The problems the world throws in your way are just challenges. Which internal voice you choose to follow is what puts you on one road or another and leads to what happens next.

However, whatever your past has been does not in any way limit what your future can be. No matter where you are in life, there is always a light to follow and a "best way to go from here." Just the tiniest change of direction can have a major effect down the road. A ten-second burst from a rocket can alter the ultimate trajectory of a space vehicle by thousands of miles. And every golfer knows that the most minute change of swing can mean the difference between landing in the fairway or in the rough. Yes, our individual nature shapes who we are and how we react to life. However, our God nature is what shapes our individual nature, and we are free to change that any time we want.

This particular letter also marks a turning point in our sharing. Until now, everything we have examined is not only documented in the *Bardo Thödol*, but has also been seen, felt, and reported on by those who have had death return experiences. What you have read so far has been verified by both ancient sages and the personal revelations of modern day travelers. However, this is the furthest extent the bardo has been penetrated and revealed by modern death return reports. Those who have come back have not told of going beyond, while those who have gone beyond have not come back to report. Modern medicine has reached its limit, at least for the moment.

Not only that, but everything which has been recounted thus far will be experienced to one degree or another by everybody, including you. This, however, is that fork in the bardo where each individual soul begins to wander off in its own direction, reaping its own rewards or facing its own music, depending on the type of life it lived on Earth. And so, even though I can say with absolute certainty what you will experience up to this point, it would be wrong to speculate on exactly what your path will be from here on in. I can only enumerate the possibilities.

Let's set the stage for what is to come by going back to what you will have experienced already. First, you would have witnessed the step-by-step separation from your body as its physical functions ceased to operate. As the body fell away you would have felt as if you were floating in a vacuum, like an astronaut moving gently through space. You would have seen the world you are leaving, but in a strangely detached manner. Eventually you would have been drawn away from the sights and sounds of Earth by an all-encompassing clear light, which would have grown and grown until it filled you completely with its presence.

That light, as you now know, is the ultimate light of creation, an aspect of what we call God. You will feel its love, warmth, and compassion, the basic elements that make up the nature of Being. They are also the basic elements that make up *your* nature, and if you feel complete, if you feel fulfilled, you will remain in that space, the space the Buddhists call nirvana, the space that we call heaven. You will be at that point where you are total perfection, and therefore all of You will be God and God will be all of You.

If you cannot hold onto the light you will meet your personal concept of ideal perfection in a living being, your yidam, your savior. That image will occupy your mind's eye, and the peace and love which fill that being will become yours. Once again, if you feel whole and complete you will merge with that, and your consciousness will experience the heaven of eternal peace and well-being. You will be the yidam, and the yidam will be you.

For the rest of our trip we have only the teachings of the *Bardo Thödol* to follow, which tell of the pathways the soul will find as it continues its journey. It has proved right thus far, and there's no reason why it should not continue to be so. Therefore it shall serve as our road map, as together we examine those pathways, what they represent, where they lead, and what the signs are by which we will recognize them.

Peace and love

26
Leaving the light

Dear friend,

Everybody while alive experiences a life that is separate from the physical, whether or not he recognizes it as such. And I'm not referring to dreams. Even the least spiritual person, the greatest seeker of physical pleasure and gratification, or the person who forces his will on others does so because he wishes to fulfill an ideal which he has already visualized on the inner screen of his mind. He may not be able to put it into words, but he has been to the world "inside" and encountered something so much to his liking that he wants to make it a physical reality as well as a mental one.

If he stops to think about it, he may call it imagination, and claim that it is unreal and nonexistent. Nevertheless, he is so sure that what he sees inside is pleasant that he rushes to reach his goal and manifest its happy ending in his lifetime. This ability to focus on an inner desire and act to create a goal in its physical form is the hallmark of the "doer," the person whom you can always count on to get the job done. Unfortunately, all this powerful energy is often directed to antisocial ends, or to "looking out for number one." It is only when that energy is teamed up with Universal Consciousness that true positive action is achieved. The rest of the time you just get a lot of people trying to reach their own goals by selling soap products to each other, or worse.

In the bardo, the clear light tests each soul's ability to merge with and hold on to the love and compassion of Universal Consciousness. From here on in each soul will follow its own path and will be tested to see how well it merges with various other basic human emotions. If you read everything that follows openly and honestly, you should be able to assess which of the emotions will be the one to lure you from the place of perfection to the "lesser neighborhoods" and ultimate rebirth. So let's start back at the light, the place we all experience, and go from there.

There will be sounds that will resonate through the radiance of the void like a thousand simultaneous thunders. "Do not be daunted, nor terrified, nor awed," says the *Bardo Thödol*. "This is merely the sound of your real Self."

The body which you will now have is a thought body, sometimes called an "astral body." It is a thought body because all the forms which you are about to see and experience are your own thought forms, that is to say, creations of your own imagination. It is important that you recognize this fact and know that you are in the world of the spirit. Once you do, you can control the visions; if you don't, the visions will control you. Now can you see the value of the meditation exercises you have been doing lately?

Since you are existing without a body of flesh and blood, nothing that may come—sounds, lights, rays, whatever—can hurt you. You cannot die. You know, it's really quite humorous how a newly deceased soul who did not expect an afterlife will flee in absolute abject fear from apparitions and visions because it is afraid of dying, not even realizing that it is already dead. The other side of that, however, is that this very failure to know and understand what is happening impels a soul in directions in which it otherwise would not wish to go, and leads it to places it would not wish to be.

The average person does not find the way out of the world of spirit via one of the two paths of clear light. In fact, the typical soul will wander from one end of the bardo to the other for a full forty-nine days, and end up later being reborn against its will, with the opportunity and challenge to "do it again until you get it right."* Meanwhile, as we have already noted, as one progresses farther and farther in the bardo from the place where the clear light leads to the eternal peace and oneness of heaven, one wanders into increasingly less pleasant neighborhoods.

Just as God represents the nature and character of the heaven of clear light, so, too, the nature and character of each section of the bardo that follows is represented by a particular deity. They are actually named and pictured, and the practitioners of Bön looked upon them as real and existing, just the same way that some Westerners view the devil as an actual being with horns and a tail. However, the Tibetan Buddhists know that these deities are truly nothing more than the creations of the mind of the deceased, as are all the monsters, gods, and apparitions which will appear as you wander through the bardo. But since you yourself do not have

_____
*The length of time believed to elapse between death and rebirth varies with different sources. For example, Theosophical literature places it at hundreds of years, while Cayce's readings often indicate less than a hundred years. Time before rebirth varies in the Tibetan teachings as well. Forty-nine days merely represents the length of the stay in the bardo, the intermediate state.—ED

a physical body, a nonphysical apparition will seem very real indeed, just as it does in a dream.

The Tibetans also recognize a kind of Soul which they call "bodhisattva," or "Buddha wisdom," for which our closest equivalent would be "saint." These are souls who have gained supreme spiritual freedom and who could have remained in ultimate God-Consciousness after death if they had wanted to. However, they have chosen to return to the world of human existence in order to share their knowledge and experience with the rest of humanity. It is hard to say how these souls will appear to the modern Westerner. They may be historical religious figures, previously deceased friends and relatives, visions of angelic forces, or wise extraterrestrials. However they are manifested, these souls will show up at various points throughout the bardo to further aid the newly deceased in choosing the proper path. What is true on Earth is true in the bardo. The soul who most needs help is least likely to follow the urging and direction of these benign spirits.

Peace and love

27
The dawning of the six realms

Dear friend,

If you lose contact with either the clear white light of perfection or the secondary clear light of your yidam, the first signs of "imperfection" begin to appear. This should occur three-and-a-half to four days after physical death—roughly the time it takes for the average person to finally accept the fact that she is, indeed, dead. These imperfections are not evils in the sense that the person who has them is "bad." Rather, they should be understood to be more in the nature of weaknesses, the forces of individuality which pull us away from God. They are the factors of personality which we all have to one degree or another and which cause us to be the people we are. These elements are ignorance, anger, ego, greed, jealousy, and stupidity.

In the Tibetan cosmology, as we have discussed, deities are used to represent each of these particular aspects of personality. And even though the personality traits they represent are negative, the deities themselves are not considered evil. Unlike our concept of Satan, these beings are not trying to lure you into error, but to lead you away from error by the very power and force of their presence. They, in fact, are known as the peaceful deities, and are the very embodiment of the triumph over personality weaknesses. If we related them to anything in our Western thought, it should be to archangels rather than devils. To those who have studied these deities throughout their lives, they present a clear and easy way for the newly deceased to know exactly where she is in her wanderings. If she can identify the deity, she can be made aware of the trait being tested and can act accordingly.

"Oh, look. There is Vajrasattva. I recognize him because he is sitting on an elephant. He is the deity who is in charge of anger and hatred. I'd better be careful. I've been known to lose my temper, and if I do so now, I could get into serious trouble."

Is that overly simplistic? Well, maybe so. But if it works, that's all that matters. Meanwhile, the Westerner, whose spirit would not conjure up these deities and who could never relate any one image with a particular personality trait anyhow, would seem to be at a loss to explain what is going on around her. However, the various points in the bardo where the individual personality traits are tested are also indicated by lights of different colors. They are shown in the following chart, and they do give you an opportunity to be aware of where you are and what is going on.

You will note that for each day spent in this section of the bardo there are two different colored lights, a bright one and a dull one. Each day also lists an emotion and a destination. The emotion is the aspect of personality being tested that day. The bright light is the radiance sent from the deity to show you the way to avoid the pitfalls of error and lead you out of the bardo to places of wonderful reward for having overcome that particular weakness. However, the *Bardo Thödol* notes that, due to their natural tendencies while alive on Earth, most people tend to avoid the glare of the bright light and lose these opportunities. How true, since if we're experiencing these lights we've already turned our back on the primary God light.

The dull lights, on the other hand, are coming from those realms where that particular personality trait is "treated," so to speak. If the soul is attracted towards these dull lights, it will end up in the locations shown, and for a period of time it will be trapped in an existence where it will experience the results of that negative emotion so strongly that it should, in theory, learn the error of its ways. While the names of some of these realms don't sound as bad as others, the *Bardo Thödol* is adamant in its universal warning to follow the bright lights and avoid the dull ones at all cost.

DAY	EMOTION	BRIGHT LIGHT	DULL LIGHT	REALM
1	Ignorance	Blue	Soft White	Devas
2	Anger	White	Smoky Black	Hell
3	Ego	Yellow	Dull Blue	Human
4	Greed	Red	Yellow/Red	Pretas
5	Jealousy	Green	Red/Green	Asuras
6	All the Above	All the Above	All the Above	All the Above
7	Stupidity	Rainbow	Green/Blue	Animals

I have tried to make the chart as simple as possible. The deities are gone, and as for the various realms, we will discuss each one in turn in future letters. Think of them not as actual locations somewhere in the physical universe, but as states of mind in which you could find yourself trapped if you are not careful. The double colors shown for three days of the dull lights are the result of disagreement among Tibetan scholars. I have been unable to determine for myself which are correct, and thus have included both. More research and study in this area should clear matters up in future editions.

Meanwhile, do not look at the chart and what it represents as being merely part of a mythology which has no bearing on you and your afterlife. While the ideas and names may be strange, the human emotions which they represent are not.

Peace and love

28
Meditation techniques

Dear friend,

The tool we have been using in these letters to prepare you for what to expect in your existence to come has been meditation, the basic exercise of yoga. This is not the kind of yoga found in health clubs that merely concentrates on pulling and stretching the body into convoluted positions. That is hatha yoga, and it is really just a preliminary step to calm and control the body so you can begin to calm and control the mind.

We have been working with jnana yoga, a discipline which views life as being more than just what appears to the physical senses while at the same time maintains that Universal Consciousness is the ultimate source of all life. This yoga speaks of the body as being only the vehicle within which our consciousness operates for the short period of time we exist on Earth. It also allows us, while living, to simulate other dimensions which our living soul will experience after the body dies. In its original form this is heavy stuff written by sages and teachers whose statements of what they knew to be true predate the findings of Moody's study of death return experiences by thousands upon thousands of years. These are writings based on ancient lines of instruction, lines which fortunately have been kept alive in the East for all these

114

years while we in the West have been denying anything we could not quantify with "scientific proof." Now the proof is in, and how marvelous it is to replace doubt with belief, and belief with knowledge.

I find it so interesting that many modern scientists who look down on anything that even hints of an inner spiritual world actually use a form of meditation to aid in solving their most difficult and complex problems. They may not call it that, but names and labels really are immaterial. Using focusing techniques in which their current research project becomes all they can see, sleep, dream, or breathe, they reach a point where all other thoughts have been eliminated from their minds. They have worked in a particular area for years and need only one little piece to be able to put the whole puzzle together. The thought of that missing element never leaves them alone. They become one-pointed in their interests, single-minded in their desires, looking to find the solution that doesn't want to come, the final answer that gives meaning to a lifetime of dedication, a lifetime of work. It may take years, it may take decades, but finally, when all logical roads lead to dead ends, with minds gone blank and burned out by the thinking process, they throw up their hands in despair and admit defeat, not focusing on anything, just plain giving up.

This combination of years of what is really the meditative act of focusing, followed by the sudden meditative act of emptying, is what produces the "aha!" moment, that sudden spark of intuition when the answer seems to fall out of nowhere. This is what happened with the discovery of the molecular structure of the benzene ring and the insight of Einstein's $E = mc^2$, as well as numerous other scientific breakthroughs throughout the ages. It also explains the next phase of meditation, one that I call *awakening*.

Not everybody who meditates experiences awakening. Some people are never able to completely still the noise inside, and so they never reach the point where complete silence reigns long enough for the next step to take place. They have worked so hard to develop their skills in logical rational thinking that they will fight to the death the idea of quieting their mind, of letting go and simply allowing the answers to flow in and fill the vacuum. Despite hints from those who have been there, they will never be still and listen to the solution that wants to come, simply because there doesn't appear to be any logical reason to do so. "Logical," of course, is equated with external in their minds, and so although they have been told that an internal door exists, they will never find it, for they continue to seek the answers by the same external processes with which they are familiar and comfortable.

You may have heard the Sunday school tale of God sitting around with the angels trying to decide where to hide from humanity:

"Why don't you hide deep down in the Earth?" one of the cherubs suggests.

"No," says God, "people will find a way to dig down for me. That's too easy."

"How about hiding in the sky?" suggests another.

"No. That's too easy, too," says God. "They will surely find a way to fly up and find me."

"I've got an idea," pipes up a third angel. "Why don't you hide inside the people themselves?"

"Great idea," says God, "they'll never think of looking for me there!"

This may sound like a cute story for third-graders, but it is true nonetheless. The door to Universal Consciousness is within each of us. It is the gateway of awakening to what is beyond limited human experience; the passageway to feeling the oneness of all life forms;

and the archway through which your spirit will pass when your body dies and you return to the Source. Quiet yourself, focus yourself, empty yourself, awaken yourself. Become familiar and at ease with the nature of the world you will one day be inhabiting.

Peace and love

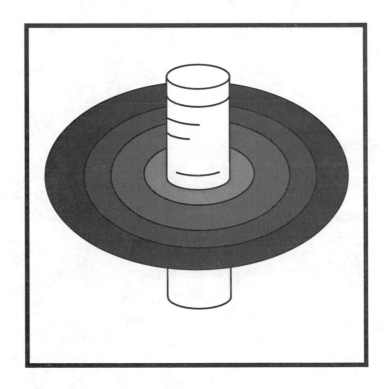

It is possible for the layers of thoughts and emotions to be so strong that you become more attached to them than you are to Universal Consciousness. "If I only could experience this," you think. And that's when you find yourself back on Earth again in another body.

29

Ignorance and anger

Dear friend,

The first day of apparitions and lights begins, on the average, three-and-a-half to four days after death. At this time your entire surroundings will appear bright blue. From a central point of this blue void will appear a being of white, from whose heart will shine a blue light so radiant and bright that you will not be able to look at it. This is the primordial light generated by the energy of total wisdom and compassion.

If you are aware at the time that this light leads in the direction of truth and ultimate peace, there is little doubt that you will follow it with complete faith and trust to its source, the origin of all things and beings. This is the point in ultimate cosmology where the undivided energy of total consciousness begins to take on individual characteristics. The Tibetans give it the colorful title of the "central realm of the densely packed"; that is, the place where all beings are combined into one prior to further separation into individual forms. To the Westerner interested in the scientific studies being done to try to trace the origin of the universe, it would correspond to the moment immediately after the big bang, when energy had converted to matter but all matter was still condensed in a minute undifferentiated mass. The big bang aside, however, the light is bright and pierc-

119

ing, and the tendency of the average soul is to avoid it out of fear of its brilliance.

Along with the piercing blue light you will also experience a dull white light generated from a source known to the Tibetans as the "realm of the devas," or gods. These are spirits of individual souls whose understanding of the true nature of existence has gotten them to the point of recognizing the benefit and purpose of a life of peace, tranquility, and meditation. They are beings who have gone beyond the gross emotions. However, they still are absorbed, as are most humans here on Earth, in the individuality of their own existence. They do not yet recognize that their souls are merely manifestations of the all-encompassing soul of the One Consciousness, that which we call God. As a result, their unwillingness to give up their personification and merge into total godhood causes them to remain in separate individual consciousness.

Devas are individual souls, good souls, peaceful souls, but not yet perfected at the level of ultimate understanding. That is the "ignorance" to which this level refers. If they could make the break and merge with the bright blue light, they would overcome that obstacle. However, if they are drawn to follow the dull white light, they will enter the world of the deva, and no matter how pleasant that seems in comparison to the experiences in the worlds to follow, it is still an obstruction on the path to ultimate liberation.

It must be reemphasized that consciousness in the bardo does not exist within a physical body and, as a result, is not encumbered by the limitations of three-dimensional experience. Therefore, "following" one light or another is not a matter of moving your feet as in this world, but rather is determined by the emotions and thought processes which you generate. Hold a vision firmly in your heart and you will be transported there.

120

Thus prayer, meditation, and the ability to focus your thoughts become the actual means of locomotion.

If you are not drawn to either of these lights, the second day a brilliant white light generated by an energy field from another point of Universal Wisdom and Consciousness will appear. Its corollary will be a dark, smoky-colored light emanating from the realm of hell. This realm is the closest thing the Tibetans have to the Western concept of Hades, and it is to be avoided at all cost. It is the abode of those who generate violence and anger and if followed, will lead to unbearable misery and suffering without any guarantee of your ever getting out.

Understand that this is not physical suffering. After all, at this time you have no physical body to undergo that type of torment. However, you do exist as a thinking, feeling being and there is no question that having to submit to mental and psychological torture would be an unpleasant way to spend the rest of eternity.

Along this line, it should be apparent by now that the attributes and characteristics which made up your personality while you were alive are the very ones which are going to make up your personality after you are dead. Therefore, you can see why the Tibetans, who have spent thousands of years studying life beyond the body, are so strong in their teachings that life on Earth is merely preparation for what comes next, and that the objects and ideas with which you most identify while alive will be the ones which will determine your ultimate destination while in the world of Spirit. If you are a person who has lived filled with anger, hatred, and violence, you will face a future of anger, hatred, and violence. If Gilbert and Sullivan's Mikado could "make the punishment fit the crime," would you expect any less from God?

Thus, you must take whatever time is remaining to

you here on Earth to train yourself in love, peace, and compassion, for if you don't, old habits of anger and hatred, practiced to perfection while in the body, may be too hard to overcome at the moment when you really need to do so. We must all learn to live our short life on Earth as if our eternal life depended on it, for in truth, it really does.

Quietly step outside of yourself and honestly look at the person you are. Have you lived life with a smile or a sneer? Do you care for others or are you only wrapped up in yourself? If you were to meet yourself for the first time, would you like you? These are not easy questions to answer, but they are real ones.

Peace and love

30
Ego and greed

Dear friend,

The third day in this section of the bardo will dawn with a bright yellow light, the transcendent brilliance of the purified element "earth." Following it and its associated figures and visions will mean that you have overcome ego and are fit to be led to an area of creation known to Tibetans as the "southern realm endowed with glory." However, this is not just a yellow brick road which you can follow at your whim and pleasure. If you are not familiar with the rules for movement in the bardo and are not adept in controlling your thoughts and emotions, you may not be able to merge with that light, even if you want to.

Its companion will be a dull blue light from the human world. Once again, the dull blue light should not be followed as it stems from the quality of ego and will lead the soul back into the human world without its having gained any knowledge from its bardo experience.

"What's so wrong with having an ego?" you may ask. "That's the very thing that makes us human. What's wrong with that?"

Of course it is only natural for you to feel that way since you are human. But this part of the bardo is designed to break through the general level of consciousness which represents the human condition. You see, the very fact of being human means that you have slipped from the ultimate point of creation where you, as total consciousness, are everything, including those things which are not defined by human limitations. Understand that just as Cro-Magnon and Neanderthal were not the ultimate ends of human development, neither are we. There are other levels of experience yet to evolve into. We're getting very subtle here, and the meaning of what I am about to say is almost more of a feeling than an understanding. Get into a gentle meditative state and see if it aids you in grasping the point.

Meditate on the sun, not as a human looking out at the sun but as if you were the sun itself. Can you feel how you give off everything you have, everything you are, your heat, your light, your energy, completely, freely, without thought of return, with no thoughts of "what's in it for me?"

Now be Earth. Feel the gifts of the sun reaching you, and feel yourself nurturing all the different forms of life which are trying to survive and grow. Feel how you do the best you can with what you have, to support and sustain all these forms in whatever way they want to develop. You both receive and give as Mother Earth.

Now meditate on the average human mentality. Feel yourself taking whatever you want from the Earth to make your life easier, to make yourself richer, to gain fame, to gain power. Feel what it is like to be a human. Feel what it is like to "look out for number one." Can you now see why I say we are not completely evolved and the human ego is not the greatest wonder in the universe?

If you are able to avoid the third day's temptations, the fourth day will shine with a brilliant red light from the element "fire." Once again it will be accompanied by visions of beings whose purpose is to aid you in escaping the wheel of individualized existence to which you are bound, in this case based on greed. But, as on the previous days, the light's radiance will cause you to turn from it, even though it leads to a place the Tibetans call the "western happy realm."

The accompanying dull light is either yellow or red and comes from a place known as the "realm of the pretas." This is the abode of greed and is symbolized in Tibetan lore by beings with very large bodies and stomachs and very small necks and mouths. Their desires may be great, but they can never get the satisfaction of filling those desires, though they spend their whole lives in that one-dimensional pursuit.

The term *pretas* has been translated as "hungry ghosts," and though the *Bardo Thödol* differentiates the "realm of the pretas" from the place we translate as "hell," its torments are very real to the spirits who exist there. Hell is hell, no matter what you call it.

Just recently a fascinating revelation struck me concerning the realm of the pretas. I was sitting outside on the kitchen patio watching spring do its thing. The early flowers were beginning to blossom, and squirrels and chipmunks raced each other across the lawn collecting acorns left over from last year. Up in the branches above my head a family of robins was moving in and, as I smiled at them over my morning coffee, I recalled reading how some birds can eat as many as five thousand insects in a single day. Driven by a need to satisfy the physical requirements of their high metabolism, they are constantly eating from the time they awaken till the time they retire to their nests at night.

I looked closer. The robins had very large bodies and stomachs but a relatively small mouth and virtually no neck at all. They fit the description of the pretas! Could it be? We sit and watch them constantly pecking, constantly searching, constantly driven for food—the robin in the garden, the swallow in the field, the pigeon chasing bread crumbs on city streets. "How cute," we think, and throw them the crusts of our sandwiches. But it is not cute to them, the inner survival force that drives them throughout their lives. Who says that the "realm of the pretas" must be located somewhere else, populated by beings unknown on Earth? Consciousness trapped inside the body of a bird that is always hungry. Off the wall? Maybe, but maybe not.

Peace and love

31
Jealousy and stupidity

Dear friend,

Onward we go through the section of the bardo presided over by the peaceful deities, where our most basic personality traits are tested. Are we tempted by baser emotions, or are we able to transcend them and follow the path of liberation of mind and consciousness?

It should be noted that the colored lights which radiate on the various days are not the actual forces that pull you down one road or another. It's not a case of saying, "Oh, blue, my favorite color. I think I'll go this way." There will be emotions associated with the lights; by creating desires and aversions within you, these feelings will impel you either towards or away from the realms which the lights represent.

Remain aware, as you pass through this area of the bardo, that from the perspective of Ultimate Consciousness which is common to all life, human language and cultural differences are immaterial. Thus, there are lessons here for everyone to learn, and though you will not be able to relate to the Tibetan images and deities that the *Bardo Thödol* describes, you will see something that evokes the same meaning for you. I have no idea what it will be. This is a new field of study in the West, and until we begin to explore the bardo with the techniques refined over millennia in the East, we will be unable to go beyond the simplest of warnings and directions in this area.

The bright light on the fifth day is green, and it is the purified form of the element "air." It is associated for Tibetans with a realm known as the "northern realm of good deeds." The emotion being examined here is jealousy, and it is interesting to note its connection with the phrase "green with envy." The accompanying dull light is either green or red, and leads to the "land of the asuras." "Asuras" is a term which has been translated as "jealous Gods." Once again, as with the land of the hungry ghosts, this is not the area of consciousness which has been translated as hell, yet it is not a place one would want to live; quarreling and warfare, says the *Bardo Thödol*, are its main characteristics.

How familiar it sounds and how easy it is to compare such a land to places on Earth where for generation after generation blood feuds and ethnic warfare have shaped and molded life into a jigsaw of pain and heartache, cruelty and suffering. How sad this concept of a jealous god whose evil impulses towards others make his own life a living hell. How sad for humans who do the same.

It is very possible, indeed probable, that a newly deceased soul, unaware of the transition awaiting it through the bardo, will avoid the bright piercing rays of wisdom sent out by its own higher consciousness in an attempt to guide it onto the proper path. Accordingly, on the sixth day, all five of the previous lights will shine at once, together with the accompanying element and deity, each from its individual compass point, with the bright light of wisdom radiating from the center. Correspondingly, the five previously seen dull lights will also appear. As you might suspect, focusing attention on them now will lead to the same unhappy fate as would have occurred had you done so the first time around.

This sixth day affords the wandering soul yet another

golden opportunity to meditate on one or another of the bright lights and merge with it, thereby achieving the liberation, or heaven, which that level of knowledge and perfection can offer. As you can see, there is no end of opportunities for you to reach a suitable destination and resting place. However, without knowing what each light represents, your choices are left to pure chance, or worse yet, to undirected fear and emotion. While it is absolutely true that a lifetime of study and knowledge is needed to know in detail all of the ins and outs of the bardo, it is certainly clear that even this single reading will give you more awareness of what you will experience after death than you would have had without it. For this I am grateful. It is the reason why this book has been written by me and by all the lamas of the past who have brought this knowledge to the point where it could be made available to you, the twentieth-century Western mind.

The seventh day is represented by a rainbow of bright colors from all the knowledge-holding deities, along with a dull green or blue light from the realm of animals. This is the abode of those who are powered and motivated by animal passions and brute feelings. It is the world of ignorance and stupidity, and should be avoided at all costs. You alone know whether such emotions would tempt you. You can also imagine the results of such an attraction.

In Tibetan folklore there is the story of a young girl who was tending her flock when an old man approached and tried, in his feeble way, to make love to her. She easily pushed him away and ran home to tell her mother. "Oh, my," said the mother after hearing his description, "that sounds like the old hermit Norbu. He is a very holy man, and if he wanted to have you there must be a very good reason. Go back and let him have his way with you."

Like a good daughter, the girl returned to the fields, and sure enough there she found old Norbu absorbed in peaceful meditation. "You may have me," she said. "I don't want you," he replied, "I never did." "Then why did you try to make love to me?" asked the girl. "Oh," answered Norbu, "the local abbot just died. He has been very derelict in his duties and studies and was about to be reborn as an animal. I hoped to provide him with a more suitable body in which to be reborn. However, it is now too late. Those two donkeys over there have just coupled and they will soon give birth to the abbot!"*

May you have better fortune.

Peace and love

---

*Although Tibetans accept such a possible rebirth as an animal, many traditions including Theosophy do not. Nevertheless, the realm of animals has real meaning for humans. —ED

32
The trek continues

Dear friend,

At this point the *Bardo Thödol* takes a break from re-counting each day's particular activity to reiterate the fact that everything experienced thus far, as well as all that is to come, is truly a creation of your own personal psyche; emanations of your own mind. This is appropriate in regard to what is about to happen.

The next set of images to be viewed is terrifying, though they are generated from the same source as those which have been appearing for the past seven days. Both are creations of your own individual personality traits and characteristics and, in fact, are designed to test the same basic emotions. Now, however, the images are manifestations of your brain and intellect, as opposed to your heart and feelings. As a result, according to the *Bardo Thödol* they are more capable of influencing you through fear, terror, and awe than those which you experienced before. But even this has its benefits, for by fearing the visions which haunt you, there is a greater chance that your consciousness will become more directed towards what is happening, and that there will be less chance of confusion. If something big and ugly is attacking, you're going to pay attention!

To the Tibetans, the deities which show up here are known as the wrathful deities as opposed to the peaceful deities which you just confronted. These entities are not evil. They are merely stronger manifestations of your own basic tendencies, and if you haven't already followed one of the lights which emanated from the peaceful deities, you once again get the opportunity to overcome your weaknesses by recognizing them in this more striking form.

These visions appear from the eighth to the fourteenth day without the accompaniment of any secondary dull lights. The original text speaks of many-headed, many-armed monsters holding skulls and drinking blood, visions designed to terrify the wandering soul of a Tibetan, although it is not certain what forms and images will be visualized by modern Westerners. It is only natural that what frightens one will not necessarily frighten another. But the visions which accompany the lights are creations of universal emotions, experienced through a particular set of individual characteristics and perceptions. The type of visual image will have to vary if it is to have the same impact on different persons, though without further study in this area we have no way of knowing what it would be for Westerners.

All that is needed at this stage of the bardo is for you to realize that everything that is happening to you is a creation of your own mind. If that thought had never occurred to you before, it's not very likely that it will now when you need it. However, that is why these letters were written and why the *Bardo Thödol* was transmitted in the first place. For if you have read and understood this text during your lifetime, so says the original, then you will surely recall it and experience the light of truth when the time comes. But if you do not realize this fact, then no matter how "religious" you have been in your lifetime and no matter how many spiritual practices you have performed, you will be forced to wander lower and lower in the bardo following the path trod by the majority of human souls, pulled ever onward by the strength of your own fears, desires, anxieties, and hangups. You will truly be creating your own reality.

In Tibet the attending lama will remain at the bedside of the deceased (whose body has long since been removed), still trying to get through to the soul wandering in the bardo. It must be extremely frustrating for the lama. He knows that if the person had paid attention to these teachings when he was alive, he would long ago have recognized some of the signposts and opted for one or another of the bright light paths to liberation which have already dawned. Yet the lama continues to read from the *Bardo Thödol* knowing that the soul he is guiding can see and hear, a fact even we now accept as a result of modern death return experiences. The hope of the lama is that at some point the soul will suddenly realize that it is experiencing the very things it heard about while alive and what it sees is all a creation of its own mind and imagination, not an external force come to harm it. The situation is akin to that of a person who is afraid upon seeing a lion, only to discover that what he's looking at is nothing but a stuffed lion's skin. If at some point the soul realizes the fact that there is nothing to be afraid of, its liberation is achieved.

Yet it need not be fear that acts as the motivator. The story is told of the stone-carver whose tiny son used to play at his feet as he went about his work carving the fierce stone images used to adorn the courtyards of temples and lamaseries. Sadly, the child fell ill and died, passing through numerous levels of the bardo in fear and terror, not knowing what was happening to him. However, the dawning of the terrifying wrathful deities brought a smile to his face. "I know who you are," he laughed. "You are the statues my father makes." Becoming at ease and merging with them, he passed through the bardo unharmed.

Thus ends the second part of the *Bardo Thödol*, dealing with the testing of our individual personality and our ability to overcome the character traits of ignorance, anger, ego, greed, jealousy, and stupidity. We entered this section from the pure realm of God and perfection, where we experienced the clear white light which is our birthright and true Self, free from all the mental and emotional encumbrances which cause pain and discomfort, misery and misfortune. We leave it clothed in all those aspects of our personality we were not able to shake off, and which, through their own force and power, will lead us to the Judgment.

Peace and love

33
Meditation techniques

Dear friend,

Awakening, as we have previously discussed, occurs at that moment when you not only notice the door inside yourself that you only suspected existed, but you find yourself standing on the other side of it without any idea of how you got there. This is something that cannot be planned, programmed, or anticipated. This is something that just happens when the quieting has been successful. It is "eureka," it is "seeing the light," but it is not necessarily "enlightenment."

You see, an awakening experience in and of itself does not mean that you have become a spiritual person. It merely means that you have touched your inner core, that part of you that is your greater consciousness and is there to serve you the answer to the particular question you had in mind. Whatever you have been focusing on—the design of benzene molecules, the relationship of mass and energy, the right word for a poem you're composing, or even the meaning of life and what happens after death—whatever answer you've been looking for will come when you pass through that door. However, if you don't recognize what has happened, and if you don't know where you've been, you'll just think, "Hey, I finally figured this out," and rush to tell everybody how incredibly clever you are.

If you think the problem was solved via your individual ego, you're going to have to go through all the steps once more to find the door again. However, if you realize that the importance of the answer you got is secondary to the internal experience you've just undergone, that's enlightenment. Then you have truly tuned in to the Universal Consciousness and can repeat the experience whenever you want. This is awareness and, to me, this is "where it's at!"

An image has recently come to mind: two equilateral triangles, one with its point facing up, and the other above it with its point facing down. They are joined where their vertices touch, like an angular figure eight or the side view of a drip coffeepot with its container for the filter on top. Your ego normally lives in the bottom triangle, the lower part of the coffee pot.

This represents your individual consciousness and is where your thinking, cognition, and conscious mental processes all take place. Intellect is measured by the size of this pot and how rapidly and deftly you can move about within it. Many people, particularly the ones who are good at it, think that the life experiences encountered in this area are the ultimate goals of existence. Of course they would think so, for they have no reason to suspect that what they are experiencing is only the bottom half of a total system.

The aspect of meditation we call quieting is aimed solely at the pot, the lower triangle, the ego consciousness. The goal is to still the ego enough so that further meditation will allow the most delicate and subtle of energies to suck your consciousness right up through the apex of the pot, right up through the paper filter and into the top section of the coffeemaker. This is the upper triangle, which is expanded or universal Consciousness. Awakening takes place the moment your awareness is raised to this level, and it can only occur when nothing at all is going on downstairs. Once the internal noise starts again, you're back down in the bottom triangle, treading coffee.

You can see, therefore, that awakening is a sudden, unexpected shot. It happens within each of us at our own pace, in our own way. Gurus gain fortunes and followings leading people to and through this spot, but in the final analysis each one's door is that individual's alone; no two people enter via the same way. Once you have been in the upper triangle, however, and have been aware of a whole new state of being and expanded consciousness, that new awareness takes over and you begin to live and understand your life from a new perspective. This is the time when you become the Sphere looking down at Flatland, the knower viewing anew the shadows on the wall of the cave. This is when you see everything which exists in the lower part of the system, where you used to spend all of your time, as being merely a reflection of a larger, more powerful inner world.

Notice that "awareness" is a passive word, unlike "quieting," "focusing," "emptying," or even "awakening." There is nothing you have to do, nothing you can do to increase your experiences in this area other than to pass once again through the connective opening of awakening and want what is available there. When you do, however, you will find some amazing things. You will find that the same upper triangle is attached to the lower triangles of all other people. You will learn that the same Universal Soul has created and powered every individual soul. You will discover that the light in one is the light in all. You will learn . . . but what good is my telling of the experiences which others have had in this place of expanded being; the final test is what you experience for yourself.

There are a number of things which can hold you back as you explore this area. The main one is fear, fear of what you may find, fear of what you are leaving behind. But knowing that death and meditation lead to the same place of expanded life should allow you to go beyond fear to find the "You" that is the most fantastic, unlimited You anyone could possibly imagine. Meditate now so that you may find the You that lives beyond the body, the You that transcends physical death, the You that knows all things, the You that is the You in all.

The Tibetans say, "To understand Life, meditate on death," for once you know what exists on the other side, you will not only truly appreciate the life you have been privileged to live, you will know better how to live it.

Peace and love

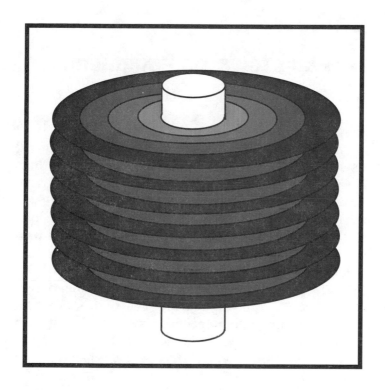

Earth is simply the physical dimension where souls who have chosen individuality get to play out their fantasies. Since each soul
has its own set of desires, there is often conflict. If each soul could
only remember that the "I Am. . ." at its core is the same as everyone else's "I Am. . ." there would be "peace on Earth as it is in
heaven."

34
Heading towards Judgment

Dear friend,

It is very possible, at least I hope it is, that you will never need to make use of the rest of what is in these letters. Way back at the beginning these writings were described as being like a road map designed to show you what you will face in the realm of consciousness which exists beyond the death of your body. As we have progressed, you have been given a number of paths and guides in the form of clear lights, bright lights, and your yidam, your own special personal conceptualization of perfection, all of which are designed to guide you through this unfamiliar and confusing maze. If you were to follow any of these paths, you would have left the bardo long before now. Let us hope that when the time comes, you do.

From here on you are entering neighborhoods in the bardo which are not as pleasant as those you have just left, places you more than likely would not want to visit voluntarily. Tibetans believe it is possible to aid the soul at any point, though it is harder to do at these lower stages. Therefore, the lamas continue to read from the *Bardo Thödol* at the empty bedside of the deceased in the hope that somewhere along the line the soul will finally realize where it is and what is happening, thereby giving it the chance to escape its fate. Its fate, as we shall soon see, is determined by the life it led on Earth. First, however, let's look at its surroundings by projecting ourselves into them.

If you reach this juncture, you will begin to feel as if you have a body, just as you did while alive. Thus, you may think that everything is as it was and you have merely been experiencing a bad dream. However, there are several signs which indicate that this is not the case. For one, any physical impairments you may have had while alive will not be present: the blind will see, the deaf will hear. The reason for this is quite logical. You are now in what we have referred to as a "thought body," an emanation of your own mind. Such a body, since it is not subject to the diseases or imperfections of the physical world, should be perfect. Your mind, in all its wisdom and imagination, would produce nothing less.

You will also begin to exhibit certain abilities which would be considered "supernatural" if they took place on earth. These include such things as being able to move instantaneously merely by thinking about where you want to be; passing through seemingly solid objects; and changing shape and size and appearing or disappearing at will. Don't get hung up on these powers and think you are special because of them. They are perfectly natural and available to everyone in the bardo where the rules of the game are different from those on Earth. But do use them as indicators of where you are and of what is going on. Remember these words and go back to focusing on the clear light or your yidam. What happens next depends on it.

The atmosphere surrounding you will be a grayish twilight type of light, with no noticeable difference between day and night. Impelled by your subconscious thoughts and desires, you will wander without any real goal or direction, the average time span in this region being twenty-two days. You may see your family and friends and try to communicate with them, but of course they will not reply and you will become depressed and downcast. Winds and storms may arise which will seem to be pushing you in a particular direction, but even though thick, awesome darkness and animal howls lie that way, you must not be afraid. Fear means you don't understand what is happening.

According to the *Bardo Thödol*, if you have led an evil life you may feel as if you are being pursued by monsters, demons, or wild beasts, all trying to kill you. Their shouts and screams will frighten you and cause you to run in panic. There may be loud sounds of thunder, crumbling mountains, and raging seas, and all these will combine to scare you to the point of absolute horror. Then, as you flee terrified, you will suddenly come face to face with three deep pits or three steep precipices, just waiting to envelop you if you should fall. One pit will be white, one will be black, and one will be red. But just as everything else you have seen is an emanation of your own mind, these are really not pits but manifestations of anger, lust, and stupidity. Avoid falling into them, but use them as road signs to recognize where you are, and pray for aid to lead you from this place. Create the vision of light or your yidam in your mind.

Of course, if you have led a good life and accumulated merit, you will not encounter the horrors described above but will find yourself impelled along the path as you experience numerous delights and pleasures. If your life has been neither good nor bad, you will just wander along indifferently experiencing neither pleasure nor pain. In any case you will be unable to stop to rest, and as a result you will feel confused and perturbed. You will try to return to your home and the people you knew in your life on Earth, but you will remain dissatisfied by your inability to make contact.

Finally, you will get the picture. The phrase, "I am dead," will cross your mind, and you'll know it to be true. Though it may seem strange as you read this now, at that time you will feel that even with the "powers" you will have at your disposal, you will want to find another body so that you can feel whole again. Such thoughts, based as they are on desire, should definitely be avoided if possible and dismissed as soon as you recognize them. For it is desires, wants, and drives that have propelled you this far in the bardo and if unrestrained will continue to lead you to places it is better to avoid.

Suddenly, you will be face to face with a deity the Tibetans call the "Lord of Death." "I will consult the mirror of Karma," he'll boom, "and check on the nature of this soul." At that time a working knowledge of karma wouldn't hurt.

Peace and love

35
The concept of karma

Dear friend,

"Every action," wrote Sir Isaac Newton, "has an equal and opposite reaction." This basic law of physics can easily be seen in the physical world, where jet planes move forward only as fast as the exhaust trails which stream out their rear, satellites are maneuvered in space by tiny, precisely measured rocket bursts, and billiard balls bounce off each other in perfect symmetry, though not always in the direction we want them to go.

We accept this law as true because we can measure its effect. We know how long to let the rocket fire in order to reach a specific orbit, and we know, at least in theory, where to aim the cue ball in order to sink the eight ball. When it comes to purely physical actions and reactions, things fall neatly into place. But there are other areas where this law is equally applicable, although it can be much harder to see and even more difficult to measure.

Karma is a way of looking at the idea of Newton's law as it relates to the actions of people, not just inanimate objects. Karma is not just an Eastern concept, although the word is newly added to our language, for the biblical teaching that you reap what you sow is exactly what karma is all about. In reality we in the West have been living with the concept of karma since the days of Moses. We just gave it a different title, calling it "cause and effect." The inability to definitely and precisely measure the effects of one's actions, however, causes some people to look askance at the whole notion. "It's all luck," they say. "Some people do little and get a lot. Others deserve more than they get. That's not reaping what you sow."

When everything else is equal, we can see the effect of karma, at least on one level. The one who puts in the greater effort usually does get the greater reward: the student who studies gets the better mark; the farmer who weeds gets the higher yield; the athlete who trains best wins the championship. When this doesn't occur, it is because conditions weren't the same at the start or varied somewhere along the way: one professor gives easier tests than another; a hailstorm hits only one side of town; one man is born with a greater ability to run for miles without getting tired. These factors may seem to produce random results, but if we could measure them and plug them into the formula the way we do with physics experiments, we would see that everything is still working precisely as it should within the law of karma. Yet, there is another area where the law holds true even though measurement is absolutely impossible.

When we approach someone with a smile, there is a greater chance that we will get one back than if we meet him with a sneer. Yet there are additional factors over which we have absolutely no control that affect the other person's reaction. We don't know on which side of the bed he got up that morning or whether he even got to sleep at all. Our smile may remind him of a certain particularly hateful relative, and could start things off on the wrong foot without either person ever knowing why. When you're dealing with people, it's impossible to predict exactly what is going to happen next. However, all things considered, a friendly approach is more likely to produce a friendly response. But this is still rather subjective, and the law of karma must rule in the objective world too if it is to be of any value.

So we appear to have something of a dilemma. The law of karma states that you will get in return whatever you give, and this appears to be so only to some extent. Yet, if we accept karma to be as true as the laws of physics, it must operate perfectly and completely. We must be able to find that missing link, that something we don't quite understand which permits gangsters to die rich and saints to be burned at the stake.

The answer lies in the fact that our lives do not end with the death of our bodies. There is still a lot of living to be done, and it is in the bardo that our recently completed physical existences will be examined to see how they affected the universal balance. That, in turn, will determine the future of our individual souls. Each and every action we undertook on Earth which has not already been counterbalanced by an appropriate reaction combines to create the karma which we take with us into the bardo. Both saint and sinner have lives that are yet to be evened up. That is what Judgment is all about. Like that billiard ball whose direction is determined by all the interactions it encounters en route to its goal, our future is based on the measurements of everything we did while alive. However, there is a major difference between us and the eight ball.

We are free to choose the direction we wish to take at every single point of our lives, but the ball is not. We can feed the beggar or kick him, steal when no one is looking or return that which we find, be instruments of war or instruments of peace. And because we are free to choose how we behave, we create the very atmosphere in which we live, and truly deserve what we get. Starting from where we find ourselves and armed with nothing more than our goals and desires and the will to

146

achieve them, we can shape not only our own lives but those of other people, people who are trying to achieve their own goals and desires. Our actions can make their lives, as well as ours, either a heaven or a hell.

Here in the bardo is where we "face the music." Now the results of our positive actions will be matched against the results of our negative actions and the bottom line read. There is no bargaining, no chance for change. For the saint and the sinner, it is as pure and immutable as the laws of physics. Each will experience the results of his or her own karma.

Peace and love

36
The Judgment

Dear friend,

We last left the Lord of Death about to look into the mirror of karma so that he might determine the quality of the soul before him and thus mete out the proper punishment or reward, as the case might be. It is a beautiful indication of the universal truth of concepts such as the last Judgment that different civilizations from different times and locations each come up with similar images. There are only minor variations based on the unique elements of their own particular culture.

In the West, we usually visualize the Judgment as taking place with some sort of scale or balance which weighs our good deeds against our bad ones while angels argue to defend our soul against the representatives of hell who act the part of prosecutor. In the Tibetan concept of the Judgment, white and black pebbles are counted out into piles, the white for good deeds and the black for evil ones. The tools of measurement are different but the idea is exactly the same. After everything is added up, the bigger pile wins.

The Tibetan also sees entities serving as prosecutors and defenders, and they are the ones who are building up the opposing piles. However, in harmony with the basic knowledge that everything is a creation of your own mind, your own self, these beings are understood to be your own good and evil elements which were created with you at the time of your birth. They are not outsiders merely taking part in someone's trial. They are you yourself, as you are and as you have lived, at your most godly and at your most human, at your best and at your worst. According to the *Bardo Thödol*, you will scream in terror as the pile of black pebbles grows. But lying or not acknowledging your evil deeds will be of no avail and the mirror of karma will be examined and your life on Earth revealed.

What the Tibetan calls the karmic mirror has been referred to in Western writing as the "akashic record." It contains an account of everything everyone has ever done while alive and your part is played back for your review in instant replay. Like it or not, you get to see yourself as you actually were, to understand the effect you had on others, to know and feel what your life meant to the world you just left. There is no hiding from the truth, for you are truth, watching the passing screenplay and comparing it to ultimate good. Your life will pass before your eyes, and you will not like everything you see.

Throughout these letters I have managed to keep from quoting from the *Bardo Thödol*; its style is pedantic and its images, as we have already discussed, are not designed for the twentieth-century Western mind. However, the emotions which the images raise are universal, and so I would like to quote from the 1927 translation just to give you some of the feeling of absolute and abject terror which the original attempts to convey. This is the point of no return. This is the place where "shouldst thou become distracted now, the chords of divine compassion of the Compassionate Eyes will break, and thou wilt go into the place from which there is no immediate liberation." The images are designed to produce such great fear and terror that the soul who faces them cannot help but finally understand and accept that indeed it is responsible for everything which it is now experiencing.

> Then the Lord of Death will place round thy neck
> a rope and drag thee along; he will cut off thy head,
> extract thy heart, pull out thy intestines, lick up thy
> brain, drink thy blood, eat thy flesh, and gnaw thy
> bones; but thou wilt be incapable of dying. Although
> thy body be hacked to pieces, it will revive again. The
> repeated hacking will cause intense pain and torture.

In truth, this picture of terror is nothing more nor less than your conscience reviewing the life you have led. Your human spirit will defend your actions: "I had to do that because of the pressure I was under." Your godly spirit will counter: "If you hadn't been motivated by base emotions, you wouldn't have been under that kind of pressure." On and on it will go, your fate hanging in the balance. Yet even here compassion reigns and you get the benefit of the doubt. Only your direct evil is counted against you, while the good done by others because of you also comes into play in your behalf.

You will experience alternating currents of momentary joy followed by momentary sorrow, brightness and void, tension and limpness. Just accept what is happening without favoring any one over the other. At this point your best mode of action, if you cannot focus on your yidam, is just to accept everything that is happening in a neutral state. Do not try to excuse yourself by finding fault in others; it will just make matters worse.

And so the trial will be held and the judgment cast. That part of you which is pure and impartial will review your life, seeing both the good you have created and the evil you have caused. Slowly you will begin to get some idea of what you will be facing, what you will have to experience personally in order to balance out the negatives which you have left behind. Six lights will begin to shine from the realms, representing the six base emotions which you had previously encountered. The colors will be the same as before, but this time there will be no bright light routes for escape. Little by little one light will begin to become more and more prominent. It is the place you will be going to pay off your karma, like it or not. The thought body which you have been using will gently begin to fade and you will know that the verdict has been rendered.

Peace and love

37
Reincarnation

Dear friend,
   The time has come to leave the bardo. It is, after all, merely a way station, a place in between. You have experienced everything it has to offer: the face to face confrontation with God as your true self, your yidam as an expression of the highest perfection you can recognize; representations of the individual base emotions which have clothed you and created the personality you have been; and last but by no means least, a replay of the life you just left. If you feel tired and exhausted, it's certainly understandable.
   If you have gotten this far into the bardo you have already passed all the rest stops and there is a karmic debt which has to be paid. The universe exists in perfect balance and harmony, and you have been allowed to see how your life has upset that balance by the way that you lived it. You yourself, while acting out the various roles during the judgment, have recognized things you did in life which could have been handled better, with greater concern for others, without causing pain in order to achieve your worldly goals. You have measured yourself against the scale of Universal Consciousness and have seen what you still have to learn. Now you will head to a life where you will face those lessons.
   Have you been guilty of anger? You will experience

a hell where anger will repeatedly be hurled against you, giving you the chance to recognize its stupidity and hurtfulness and to grow to overcome it in your own being. Has your life been shaped by greed and avarice? You will wake up in the world of the pretas, your existence dominated by insatiable desires that can never be fulfilled, until you finally realize that the goal of life, ultimate happiness, comes from within, not by the mere accumulation of material things. Have you been dominated by ego? Has your life been strictly a case of "looking out for number one," everyone else be damned? You will be returned to that realm where overcoming ego is the lesson that must be learned. You will be condemned to be reborn as a human being!

Life, you see, is not just a one-shot deal; the universe is more forgiving, more loving than that. Do you pay for your errors? Yes, you do. Will you reap as you sow? Absolutely. Does the law of karma work as perfectly and precisely as the laws of physics? Yes, it does. But you will not be condemned for all time in a fiery furnace without the chance to redeem yourself. Thankfully, mercifully, you will be given the opportunity to "try again until you get it right."

Reincarnation is not a new idea; over half the world's population accepts it. Even here in the West, where orthodox doctrines have tended to suppress it, the doctrine has surfaced repeatedly in the writings of seers and philosophers of all ages, including Plato, Walt Whitman, Henry David Thoreau, Victor Hugo, and numerous others since. Many of the early Christian writings include references to reincarnation, and they were accepted as revealing true teachings of Jesus until they were declared heretical hundreds of years after his death. Knowledge of karma and the revelations of the bardo should now give you the ability to see and understand reincarnation from the larger perspective.

Would you inflict harm on others if you knew, really knew, that you would be repaid in kind? Would you rob, kill, or rape if you had not the slightest doubt that you would be robbed, killed, or raped in turn? That seems much more logical than an amorphous eternal hell where all souls face the same fate no matter what their crimes. Such a scenario as hell may make it easier to separate things into black and white, facilitating judgment by Earthbound courts. But it is based on fear and the concept of a God of retribution rather than on love and a God of compassion. Compassion says pay for your crimes but then be pardoned. Even our imperfect human society does that. Does this mean we are more compassionate than God? No, it cannot be, for our compassion is a mere reflection of Infinite Compassion. Reincarnation provides the method for Divine Compassion to teach us and to raise the level of human consciousness, leading to the eventual creation of heaven on Earth, as life was truly meant to be.

Reincarnation also logically explains the implementation of the law of karma: why some seem to get the breaks. The explanation is that she earned it! Also, logically how can a soul face an eternal future but a finite past? It can't. You have been here before and you'll be here again! Reincarnation is real.

Meanwhile, back in the bardo, as a witness to your own Judgment you will be open to the Universal God-Consciousness that lets you see yourself as you truly are, the Consciousness that first made its presence known as the clear light at the moment of death. As your thought body begins to fade and the signs of the place where you will soon be born grow brighter, you will feel your own compassionate heart and will know that, in truth, all life is one. How great is the remorse you will feel? It will be as great as the remorse of God for hurt done to any of his creation. For at that moment you will know the truth. You are God, we all are God. Each of us has the same universal core of perfection, just covered by the individual nature of our own personal free will. You will see all and you will know all, and you will vow to live the rest of your eternal existence in this state of unbounded bliss and unlimited ecstasy, dedicating yourself to the good of all sentient beings.

But your next life will beckon, and you will see beings of the sort you will soon become. The realization will hit you that this beautiful place of infinite God-Consciousness will soon be forgotten and your mind trapped in the finite skull of the body in which your sentence is to be served and your lessons learned. You may feel despair, but there is yet a final escape possible.

Peace and love

38
Choosing the right rebirth

Dear friend,

The journey through the bardo is almost over. Various signs will now appear giving a clue as to where you are headed. According to the *Bardo Thödol*, the world of the devas is indicated by temples and mansions of precious metals; that of the asuras by a forest or circles of fire; that of animals by rock caverns and deep holes; that of the pretas by treeless plains, forest wastes, and jungle glades; hell by black and white roads and houses and gloom, accompanied by the sound of wailing. Of these, only the world of the devas is safe to enter.

The human world, according to Tibetan teachings, is indicated by four different continents, three of which project images of lakes, one with horses, one with cattle, one with swans. The fourth continent is represented by great mansions similar to those of the devas, and is recommended over the others because it gives the opportunity for spiritual advancement. How Westerners will experience these worlds can only be speculated upon at this point in time.

All around you will be hidden doorways leading to rebirth in the place and form suitable for the fulfillment of all the karma you have created, not only in your last life but in earlier ones as well. They may not look like doors, but indeed they are, leading to yet another round in the inevitable cycle of birth, death, and rebirth. The less mastery you have of your thoughts and emotions at this time, the more you will be impelled to enter one of these doors by forces you feel are outside your control. If you enter, you are lost.

Strong winds may buffet you, lightning strike, thunder crash, and rain and hail beat down in icy torrents. You may squeeze into a crevice in a rock wall to escape the downpour, only to find yourself trapped. Or you may be on an open plain being chased by wild beasts and demons beyond description. A jungle may loom ahead and you may enter, hoping to hide from your pursuers. You push your way into the thickest, densest undergrowth you can find. Silently, stealthily, the vines wrap tightly around you and you are trapped. The possibilities of mind are endless.

Pushed and pulled by your desires and aversions, you will have been led unwittingly to that place in the bardo where you can no longer move freely by mere thought alone. The tie to your next physical life has been made, your consciousness has merged with a new body, and in a little while you will be born into your new life. The hiding place you chose in the bardo becomes the womb that spits you out into the physical world. It's time to go around again.

"Stop!" says the *Bardo Thödol*. These drives, these desires, these attractions and aversions—haven't you learned yet that they are the cause of all your misery and unhappiness? Here you are trying to get away from some pursuer which you should know by now is just your own mental creation, and you end up getting stuck in a womb somewhere about to be reborn to God knows what kind of life. Remember your yidam, see the light, focus on the illusion of your pursuers. This is your last chance!

It is also possible that you will see visions of a couple

in sexual union. If you are to be reborn male, you will feel attraction for the female and hatred for the male. If you are to be reborn female, the feelings will be reversed. You may watch them mate, and as they achieve orgasm, you will faint into unconsciousness. When you revive, it will be in the body physically formed by that union. Once again your desires will have gotten you into a mess that will literally take you a lifetime to undo. According to the *Bardo Thödol*, such birth can be avoided by remaining neutral and not letting your feelings cause you to favor either the male or the female until the vision passes.

But practically speaking, the possibility of avoiding rebirth this close to the finish line is slim at best. Nevertheless, here is one more bit of advice, one final attempt to aid the soul whose karmic tendencies are rushing it headlong into another lifetime of being assailed by the winds of outrageous fortune. Since rebirth can't be avoided, at least here's how to choose which womb to enter.

You may begin to perceive a sweet-smelling sensation and be attracted to it. Certain visions may come to you, in which one birth may appear good and another bad. However, because of your prior karma, the very opposite may be true. In other words, do not trust your own thoughts and do not be drawn by them in one direction or another. Rather, determine to be born in a highly evolved position where you can dedicate and devote your life to the good of all sentient beings. With those pure thoughts in your mind, you can safely enter the womb that is drawing you to it knowing that you will be embarking on a good and worthwhile life. And if you can remain alert and aware enough to bless the womb as you enter, visualizing it as a celestial mansion and bathing it in pure clear light, it couldn't hurt.

❄   ❄   ❄   ❄   ❄

And so the reading of the *Bardo Thödol* by the bed-side of the deceased is over. The lama picks up his wooden bowl and staff and, paying respects to the family he has been living with for the last forty-nine days, he leaves the house and climbs back up the slope to the lamasery. There he will continue his daily life of prayer, study, and meditation until the next time someone in the village dies. The family is glad to see him go. It's nice to have one less person to cook for, and one less sleeping mat on the floor. Somewhere in the universe a soul fares better because of the actions of the lama. Somewhere in the future the world fares better because of the actions of that soul.

Peace and love

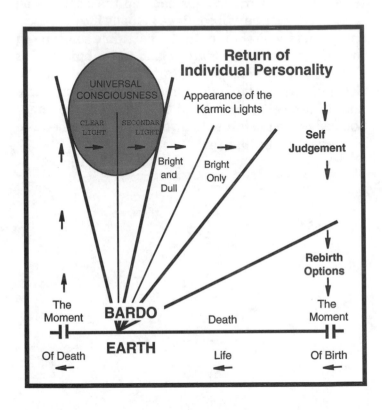

Consciousness is always alive, whether we are in a physical body or not. At the moment of death we leave our current body and enter the bardo, where we experience the clear light and perfection of Universal Consciousness. If we have karmic debts to repay, or if our desires pull us back, we return again in a never-ending cycle of birth, death, and rebirth. Only by transcending the sense of separate self and merging with Universal Consciousness can we end the cycle.

39

I hear you are about to be reborn

Dear friend,

I hear you are about to be reborn, and I'd like you to understand what is about to happen.

First of all, you must know that you are not alone. Almost all souls who have ever assumed a physical form get reborn. Those who have passed through life with the limited awareness of flowers are reborn with the slightly more advanced awareness of trees. Those who have experienced life as reptiles are reborn as mammals. Those who were humans, because of their gift of free will, are reborn either higher or lower, based on how they have lived their previous lives.

Rebirth is a natural thing. The moment you die you are condemned to rebirth, unless, of course, you finally break the cycle and merge with Oneness. That's just the way it goes, like it or not. Continue to identify with an individual ego, and rebirth in one form or another will occur. It's nature's way of getting you to evolve.

Even though rebirth is only a physical thing, it is the key to your development as a completely evolved soul. When that first desire for experience rippled across the stillness of your being, when that initial "what if?" crossed the vastness of your infinite mind, when one

161

small part of you chose to separate from your totality to "see what it's like to be out on your own," you entered a self-made world of physical senses and sensations designed to lure and tempt you away from who you truly are. That is what happens in the physical world. It is never a question of if in the physical world; it is only a question of how far.

But life is more than a physical thing. Here, between births, your consciousness is aware of the power in the heart of a seed that can make it grow into a tree. You know that life is not money or fame or power or looks, that physical attributes do not make one more or less human. You know that love lives within your own heart and that happiness is there as well, if you only know how to find it. And you know that you are always You, whether you remember it or not.

Here, between births, your consciousness needs no proof in order to know the truth. It has existed within each of us always, though it is often forgotten when we walk on the planet designed to receive us in our physical form. Those who have felt this inner knowledge while alive have been called fools and children, philosophers and lovers. Yet this is truly the knowledge of life.

The greatest teachers throughout the history of Earth have been those who taught this knowledge. They have affirmed that life is found within, that life is more than death. They could not prove scientifically what they knew, for proof, like death, is a physical thing, while life transcends the physical world and physical proof. Yet many lost their lives because of the words of their hearts, sacrificing their bodies rather than lying.

You are about to reenter the physical world, a realm where souls become so attached to the senses that they forget that life exists beyond the death of the physical body.

Life beyond rebirth is different from life before birth.

162

As a result, the ways of living, moving, and communicating which you have learned and adapted to during your stay in the bardo will not necessarily apply in the realm of your new existence. You will be a newborn babe when your life force enters a physical body, as exposed to the reality of that other world as someone newly dead is in entering this one. I could tell you what those differences will be, but you will probably forget everything at birth anyway.

The truth of life is eternal. It was accepted on Earth as long ago as twelve hundred years, in the revelations of Padma Sambhava, founder of Tibetan lamaism; two thousand years ago, in the teachings of Jesus of Nazareth; and twenty-six hundred years ago in those of Gautama, the Buddha. It is thirty-five hundred years old, in the words revealed by Moses, and as old as humanity itself in the techniques of yoga, which permit the Earthbound soul to go inside its very being to find that part of itself that lives forever.

But even though the truth has been taught for millennia, it is only within the lifetime of those now on the planet that this widely scattered knowledge has come together and been related to the truth that lives within each individual Self. This is because it is only within this same time frame that Earthbound medical science has been able to resuscitate patients from the ranks of the clinically dead, patients who have reported the exact experiences the ancient texts predicted. Think of it! The truth has always been there in the grasp of every soul, yet humanity has accepted this knowledge only when the answers came from outside instead of inside. What poor fools not to use our own inner powers.

The truth of life beyond death has not yet been incorporated into the traditional Western religions as they are known today. Yet I feel sure that within one generation it will be common knowledge, and the subject of open acceptance in the most conservative and orthodox of churches. Meanwhile, a New Age is developing on Earth, made up of individuals of all faiths who have found this inner knowledge not only augments their previous beliefs, it is now the basis of them.

Life in a body exists in one form or another for all souls with unfulfilled karma, no matter what they believe. Open your mind to this fact when one day, once again, you awaken inside a cramped and limited physical body. It may help you to make the best of the situation. May these words help you when that day comes.

Peace and love

The Hundred Syllable Mantra

Om vajrasattva samayamanu palaya
Vajrasattvatvenopatishtha
Dridho me bhava, Sutoshyo me bhava
Anurakto me bhava, Suposhyo me bhava
Sarva-siddhim me prayaccha,
Sarva-karmascu ca me cittam shreye kuru

Hum! ha ha ha ha hoh!
Bhagavan Sarvatathagata vajra
Ma me muncha! Vajri bhava!
Mahasamayasattva ah hum phat!

OM. With the vow of your incorruptible being
Keep watch over me, oh Vajrasattva,
Stay near me, steady me, gladden me,
strengthen me, be loving unto me,
Bestow upon me all perfections
and grant me pure virtue in mind and deed.

Hum! ha ha ha ha hoh!
Blessed ones, already perfect ones
Please do not abandon me!
Give me a will of steel
You, who have sworn to help all beings!
Ah Hum Phat!

Suggested Readings

Aries, Philippe. *Western Attitudes Toward Death: From the Middle Ages to the Present*. Baltimore: Johns Hopkins University Press, 1974.

Bach, Richard. *Illusions*. New York: Dell, 1977.

Benson, Herbert. *The Relaxation Response*. New York: William Morrow and Company, 1975.

Bentov, Itzhak. *Stalking the Wild Pendulum*. New York: Bantam Books, 1977.

Bloomfield, Harold H., et. al. *TM: Discovering Inner Energy and Overcoming Stress*. New York: Delacorte, 1975.

Burtt, E. A., ed. *The Teachings of the Compassionate Buddha*. New York: Mentor Books, 1955.

Collins, John J. and Michael Fishbane, eds. *Death, Ecstasy, and Other Worldly Journeys*. Albany, NY: SUNY Press, 1995.

David-Neel, Alexandra. *Magic and Mystery in Tibet*. New York: Dover Publications, 1971.

Ellwood, Robert. *Finding the Quiet Mind*. Wheaton, IL: The Theosophical Publishing House, 1983.

Evans-Wentz, W. Y. *The Tibetan Book of the Dead*. London: Oxford University Press, 1927.

Freemantle, Francesca and Chogyam Trungpa, eds. *The Tibetan Book of the Dead*. Boulder, CO: Shambhala, 1975.

Gordon, David Cole. *Overcoming the Fear of Death*. Baltimore: Penguin Books, 1970.

Grof, Stanislav. *Manuals for Living and Dying*. New York:

Thames and Hudson, Inc., 1994.

Grof, Stanislav and Christina Stanislav. *Beyond Death.* London: Thames and Hudson, 1980.

Gyatso, Tenzin, The Fourteenth Dalai Lama. *Kindness, Clarity, and Insight.* Ithaca, NY: Snow Lion Publications, 1984.

Hampton, Charles. *The Transition Called Death.* Wheaton, IL: The Theosophical Publishing House, 1943.

Hesse, Hermann. *Siddhartha.* New York: New Directions, 1951.

Hodson, Geoffrey. *Through the Gateway of Death.* Adyar, Madras, India: The Theosophical Publishing House, 1953, 1986.

Kastenbaum, Robert. *The Psychology of Death.* New York: Springer, 1992.

Kellehear, Allan. *Experiences Near Death.* New York: Oxford University Press, 1996.

Kübler-Ross, Elisabeth. *On Death and Dying.* London: Collier-Macmillan, 1969.

Leadbeater, C. W. *The Life After Death.* Adyar, Madras, India: The Theosophical Publishing House, 1912, 1986.

Levine Stephen. *Meetings at the Edge.* New York: Bantam Doubleday, 1984.

Lilly, John C. *The Center of the Cyclone.* New York: Bantam Books, 1973.

Liverziani, Filippo. *Life, Death, and Consciousness.* Bridport, England: Prism Press, 1991.

Lodo, Venerable Lama. *Bardo Teachings, The Way of Death and Rebirth.* San Francisco: KDK Publications, 1982.

Lusseyran, Jacques. *And There Was Light.* Boston: Little, Brown and Company, 1963.

Meek, George W. *After We Die, What Then?* Columbus, OH: Ariel Press, 1987.

Monroe, Robert A. *Journeys Out of the Body.* Garden City, NY: Doubleday & Co., 1971.

Moody, Raymond A. *Life After Life.* New York: Bantam Books, 1975.

_____ . *Reflections on Life After Life.* Harrisburg, PA: StackpoleBooks, 1977.

Muktananda. *Does Death Really Exist?* South Fallsburg, NY:

SYDA Foundation, 1981.

Mullin, Glenn H. *Death and Dying, The Tibetan Tradition.* Boston: Routledge & Kegan Paul, 1986.

Nugent, Christopher. *Mysticism, Death, and Dying.* Albany, NY: SUNY Press, 1994.

Pagels, Elaine. *The Gnostic Gospels.* New York: Vintage Books, 1981.

Pearce, Joseph Chilton. *The Crack in the Cosmic Egg.* New York: Pocket Books, 1973.

_____. *Magical Child Matures.* New York: E. P. Dutton, 1985.

Pelgrin, Mark. *And a Time to Die.* Wheaton, IL: The Theosophical Publishing House, 1962.

Perkins, James S. *Through Death to Rebirth.* Wheaton, IL: The Theosophical Publishing House, 1961.

Prabhavananda, Swami and Christopher Isherwood, eds. *The Song of God, Bhagavad-Gita.* New York: Harper and Brothers, 1944.

Ram Dass. *Be Here Now.* San Cristobal, NM: Lama Foundation, 1971.

Ramakrishna, Sri. *Teachings of Sri Ramakrishna.* Hollywood: Vedanta Press, 1975.

Reanney, Darryl. *After Death.* New York: William Morrow, 1991.

Rinbochay, Lati and Jeffrey Hopkins. *Death, Intermediate State and Rebirth in Tibetan Buddhism.* Ithaca, NY: Snow Lion Publications, 1985.

Ring, Kenneth. *Life at Death: A Scientific Investigation of the Near-Death Experience.* New York: Coward, McCann & Geohegan, 1980.

Ring, Kenneth. *The Omega Project.* New York: William Morrow, 1992.

Robinson, James M., ed. *The Nag Hammadi Library.* San Francisco: Harper & Row, 1978.

Rosenthal, Ted. *How Could I Not Be Among You?* New York: Avon Books, 1975.

Sabom, Michael B. *Recollections of Death.* New York: Harper and Row, 1982.

Sogyal, Rinpoche. *The Tibetan Book of Living and Dying.* San Francisco: Harper Collins, 1993.

Steinbach, Richard. *Why We Live After Death.* Gambier, OH:

169

Grail Foundation Press, 1996.

Tatz, Mark and Jody Kent. *Rebirth: The Tibetan Game of Liberation*. Garden City, NY: Anchor Press/Doubleday, 1977.

Thomas, Lowell. *Out of This World*. New York: The Greystone Press, 1950.

Watts, Alan. *The Book*. New York: Vintage Books, 1972.

White, John. *A Practical Guide to Death and Dying*. Wheaton, IL: The Theosophical Publishing House, 1980.

Williams, Paul. *Das Energi*. New York: Warner Books, 1978.

Yogananda, Paramahansa. *Autobiography of a Yogi*. Los Angeles: Self-Realization Fellowship, 1977.

Zaleski, Carol. *Otherworld Journeys*. New York: Oxford University Press, 1987.

Zweig, Paul, ed. *Muktananda: Selected Essays*. New York: Harper & Row, 1976.

Testimonials from Readers of *Letters To A Dying Friend*

"I have just finished your recent book, *Letters To A Dying Friend,* and have found it to be enlightening, helpful, instructive, and comforting. I am a nurse midwife and wish to purchase three more books to share with my patients."—JKM

"I have read several books dealing with the afterlife including Plato's Dialogues, Seth material, and the Bible. Your book helped to pull all the bits and pieces of what I have been feeling and reading into a meaningful direction. Thanks."—J

"Although I had read *The Tibetan Book of the Dead* a few years ago, it was *your* book that clarified what I had read before. Thank you for writing *"Letters"* and I wish you the very best with your important work."—ME

"*Letters To A Dying Friend* really 'blew my mind.' It made me understand the complex *Book of the Dead,* which I read but could never put to practical use. The simplicity with which you wrote made it almost seem that you were guided."—AS

"I'm very curious about 'what comes next.' Who isn't?"—JRC

"I have found *Letters To A Dying Friend* to be very enlightening and have begun daily meditation as suggested in the book. My first experience in meditating produced beautiful pastel colors which helped to relax me. Please send a copy of your book to my daughter and her husband."—PAS

"I have been diagnosed with terminal cancer. *Letters To A Dying Friend* can't change that, but it has relieved my fears and put my mind at peace for the journey I am about to take. Thank you for writing it. Peace and love to you, too."—RA